Leadership

excellence
BY DESIGN
Leadership

The Six Key Characteristics
of Outstanding Leaders

SECOND EDITION

John B. Spence

FLYCASTER & CO.

Flycaster & Company
14722 NW 140St
Alachua, FL 32615

Originally published by Flycaster & Company, 2001.
Second Edition published by Flycaster & Company, 2008.

Printed in the United States of America

Book Design by Flycaster & Company

Excellence By Design: Leadership

The Six Key Characteristics
of Outstanding Leaders

SECOND EDITION

Contents

Why You Should Read This Book

If you want to become a better leader—in your business, your community, your volunteer position, your family, or even your life—this book is for you. This book cuts through clutter and focuses only on the fundamentals—the specific ideas, tools, and behaviors that you must adopt to become a more successful leader, regardless of whom you lead. My goal is to give you a book that you can read quickly, with ideas you can learn to apply immediately, for strong positive impacts on your personal and professional life.

In my current role as a management consultant and corporate trainer to organizations across the globe, I've made a career of taking massive amounts of information on a given topic and spending weeks or months studying it in depth. I then boil all the material down to the bare essentials and present those key points in speeches, seminars, or multi-day workshops.

This book is built on that same model; it's a distillation of thousands of hours of research, hundreds of surveys, and many years of professional observation of what it takes to be an excellent leader.

I don't claim that this book will shock you with dramatic and revolutionary new leadership theories. In fact, if you were to read 400 other books on leadership and condense their main ideas, you would uncover a set of common principles—a distinct pattern that I'll call "The Absolutes of Leadership." What I have done here is to outline those principles for you in a clear, straightforward, brief, realistic, and applicable manner.

I'm not trying to reinvent the leadership wheel— I just want to help you get your wheel running as smoothly and effectively as possible, and save you about ten years of reading!

Why I Wrote Excellence By Design: Leadership

I don't think it is particularly important that you know my entire life history, but I've had an eclectic professional career that has played a unique role in determining how and why I wrote this book. If I share a few highlights of my background—especially those that have had major impacts on my reasons for producing this work—it will help you better understand the information and how it's presented, and give you a sense of how my thoughts and ideas developed.

John Goes to Work

Two years before I graduated from college, I decided that my life's ambition was to get paid to travel around the world, fish in exotic locations, lie on the beach enjoying rum drinks, and get a really good tan.

I announced this plan to my friends, who laughed; my professors, who laughed even harder; and my family, who laughed hardest of all—except for my dad, who found no humor at all in my plan.

Upon graduation, I accepted a position as Director of Development and Communications for The Billfish Foundation, a marine conservation organization founded by one of the Rockefellers. Essentially, my job was to travel around the world to marlin fishing tournaments, spend a week or two with very wealthy people on their sportfishing yachts or playing golf, and persuade them to make significant contributions to fishery conservation.

Ha, ha! I'd done it—gotten my dream job. This experience was one of my first big lessons on the power of vision and the value of planning.

But just a few years later, I had a rude awakening from my dream. Through a series of business crises, a managerial reorganization, and some improbable timing, at the age of 26 I found myself promoted to Executive Director of The Billfish Foundation.

Just three years out of college, and I'd been put in charge of a company that had on its board some of the most successful men in the world. The net worth of the foundation's combined directors stretched into billions of dollars. Winthrop (Win) Rockefeller was the president and chairman, Donald Tyson of Tyson Foods was the treasurer, and the rest of the board was sprinkled with multimillionaires and celebrities, including golfing legend Greg Norman. This board expected excellence and was accustomed to success. I had a lot of learning to do—fast.

My direct supervisor at the foundation was Win Rockefeller, an absolutely wonderful man who taught me a great deal, but who was far too busy to manage personally a young executive who needed day-to-day coaching.

Luckily, Mr. Rockefeller had the foresight to point me in the direction of a talented and patient mentor—his right-hand man at the time, Charlie Owen. Charlie was a lawyer, accountant, strategic planner, and trusted counselor, all rolled into one.

Whenever one of Win Rockefeller's 20-plus business ventures needed attention, he sent in Charlie; if he wanted to acquire a new company or major asset—in went Charlie; find or fire a CEO for one of the WinRock companies—call Charlie. To get that young kid Spence, who doesn't even know where to sign a paycheck, up to speed—sounds like a job for Charlie.

Charlie intimidated me. He was one of the most brilliant, and at times most demanding, businessmen I had ever met. He had a laser-like focus, an ability to give uncanny attention to even the minutest details, and an IQ that must have been off the charts. And, as I began to discover, he was also a great teacher.

I found out that Charlie had a son about my age, who had just left home to study in England. Charlie loved his son, and missed him terribly. So for a few years, Charlie adopted me—teaching me everything he wanted to teach his own son. I will always be better for that experience.

Our first lesson began when he pulled a book out of his briefcase and placed it on the corner of my desk. "You might want to take a look at that, John," he said casually. "It has a few good ideas in it."

Later that week, during our trip to the local diner for chili day, Charlie asked what I thought about the book. I knew it had been a test and I'd read every page, highlighter and pen in hand. For the next hour or so, we discussed the merits of the text, what I had learned, and, specifically, how I would apply what I'd learned to running The Billfish Foundation. As we got up to leave, Charlie reached into his briefcase and handed me another book. "This might fill in a few of the holes," he said.

So it began, with Win or Charlie giving me a different book to read each week. Most of the time they recommended business books, but there was the occasional philosophy tome, with a little physics, history, law, and poetry thrown in for balance. That's how I developed the habit of regular, extensive reading. Over the past dozen years, I've tried to push myself a little harder than just 50 books a year; I shoot for reading 80-100 educational or business books a year, and listening to another 30 or so audio books.

The other way that Win and Charlie taught me was the best way—by example. I would be sitting at my desk working, when a call would come through from Charlie at the Rockefeller headquarters in Little Rock, Arkansas. "We're negotiating the Allied deal this Thursday," he might say. "I want you to sit in and observe." I'd jump on the corporate jet and travel to some distant boardroom to watch silently as accomplished businessmen put together massive deals. Afterward, Charlie would pull me aside and we'd spend hours going over every detail of the meeting. "Why do you think they said so and so?" he would ask me. "What would you have done if...?" "Do you realize they forgot to ask about...?"

No MBA program in the world could offer the education I was getting. I learned some amazing lessons from Win and Charlie in those days—lessons that I will try to pass along to you in this book.

My Life as a Consultant

After several years as the director of The Bill-fish Foundation, my team had more than doubled the size of the organization and expanded membership into 26 countries. I was beginning to get burned out, however, and decided it was time to try something new.

For a few years, a gentleman I'd met at a Virgin Islands marlin-fishing tournament had been trying to convince me to work for him. He was the president of a leading consulting firm that specialized in high-level strategic sales training—helping the sales teams of Fortune 500 companies learn how to prepare fully when attempting to close mega-million-dollar deals. He said he was ready to retire to his yacht in the Bahamas, and wanted me to take over the firm. I knew almost nothing about sales, training, or consulting, but it sounded like fun, so I took the job.

The day I started, I was immediately sent out on assignment. For the next eight months, I went from company to company, sitting and watching as the firm's partners ran some of the top sales and management teams in the world through their paces. In a typical week, we would work on projects totaling as much as $100 million.

Within the firm, all partners were rated according to their proficiency at teaching the various topics in which we specialized. A junior partner like me would start as a "C" level instructor. At that level of competency, I was not allowed to teach, only to observe and study. At the "B" level, an instructor was assigned just a few modules to present. An "A" level instructor was required to be expert in delivering the dozens of classes our firm offered. The training process was arduous, and many high-level executives never made it to "A" level.

For me, getting to "A" level meant reading more than 300 books on sales, management, and strategic planning; memorizing almost 700 slides; and spending endless hours trying to improve my presentation skills. I was able to make the grade, but my very quick "Tasmanian devil" presentation speed often put my prized "A" status in jeopardy.

I spent only a few years with this firm before launching my own consulting business, but I learned some valuable lessons. The most important thing I came to realize was that if you pick one subject and study it with great zeal for several months, you can become pretty darn knowledgeable. For example, I was recently hired by a large corporation to teach professional negotiations to their entire management team. I already knew a fair amount about negotiating, but not enough to stand up in front of the senior managers of this Fortune 100 company and teach them for an entire day. So I went to three different bookstores and bought every single book they had on negotiations, then spent two weeks reading and marking each book from cover to cover—twice. Next, I bought every audiotape I could find on negotiating, then spent more than 80 hours listening and taking notes. For over a month, from sunup to sundown, I did nothing but study the arts and skills of professional negotiating.

When I was finished, I condensed all of that information (about 3,000 pages) into a 40-page outline of the key themes I had gleaned from those books and audiotapes. This process did not necessarily make me the world's leading expert on professional negotiations, but combined with my years of experience in the corporate world, I felt much more knowledgeable about negotiating than the average businessperson—and definitely qualified to lead a one-day training session on the topic.

Over the past 10 years, I have repeated this process several times. I pick a subject, whether strategy, consultative sales, leadership, conflict resolution, advanced interpersonal communications, high performance teams, or whatever sounds interesting or is requested by a client—and immerse myself in it for several months at a time.

What happens during that process is almost magical. As I read, study, reread, and compare notes, I start to see patterns. Key themes appear over and over. Some themes are subject-specific—the core elements of particular topics. Other themes are more universal—regardless of the subjects, they seem to run like threads through all patterns of thought. Themes such as honesty, integrity, values, focus, self-examination, striving for excellence, and the importance of vision are common to every discipline that I have studied.

As I said in the introduction, this book will help you discover, learn, and reaffirm those types of key universal principles as you design your personal philosophy of leadership excellence.

The Inspiration for This Book

The *aha!* experience that convinced me to write this book happened in a unique setting. Imagine sitting down to dinner with 40 or so of the nation's most successful entrepreneurs and corporate icons, and listening as each of them talks at length about what made them so successful. In 1997, I had just such an opportunity. I was invited to the ultra-elegant Breakers Hotel in Palm Beach, Florida, to attend a very special event honoring some of

America's greatest business leaders.

Since 1981, Northwood University has annually selected a handful of people to receive the prestigious Outstanding Business Leaders Award in recognition of their careers and accomplishments as modern heroes and heroines of enterprise. People such as Mary Kay Ash, Herb Kelleher, Arnold Palmer, W. Clement Stone, Dave Thomas, and dozens more equally successful people have been so honored. In attendance that evening in 1997 were the chairmen, CEOs, and presidents of a number of Fortune 500 corporations, as well as their counterparts from dozens of our country's most successful private companies. For someone like me, who's made a career of studying leadership and success, the chance to meet and talk with these executives was a rare opportunity indeed.

My greatest thrill came at the end of the evening, when I was presented with a special volume containing the acceptance speeches of more than 150 past recipients of the Northwood Outstanding Business Leaders Award. Here, in their own words, these accomplished individuals reflected about the reasons for their extraordinary success.

As I read and reread their stories, a distinct pattern emerged. Although the leaders came from every imaginable industry, ranged in age from 34 to 89, had 100 or 100,000 employees, and were born rich or poor, each of their essays touched on the fundamental criteria needed to become an outstanding leader. What was more amazing was that these criteria were the same principles that had emerged during my years of study and professional experience.

This book is about those criteria for success— the six key characteristics of all excellent leaders.

Go for the Gold

On the following pages, you'll discover some amazing ideas—even life-changing ideas. You are already familiar with many of these ideas, and you'll nod your head and smile as you read them. You may find other ideas startling or confusing, and you may question them.

I have taught these leadership skills and characteristics to more than 300,000 people around the globe and, almost universally, everyone sees the power and truth in them. So all I ask is that you keep an open mind and ask yourself: **"How can I use this information? What does it mean to me and my life? How can I apply these ideas to the way I lead in my organization?"**

I'm not saying that everything in this book is 100 percent right for every person who reads it—these are simply observations, ideas, and suggestions. Most of this material has been gleaned from the very best thinkers in the world as well as from my personal experience working with many of the top companies around the globe—but to be relevant, the ideas must make sense to you.

Regardless of the kind of organization in which you work, or whom you aspire to lead, I have tried hard to ensure that you will find useful and valuable ideas in the following pages. So read, take notes, and contemplate. There are nuggets of pure gold waiting to be found in this book—enjoy the search!

1
Dream Big Dreams

"We grow great by dreams. All big men are dreamers. They see things in the soft haze of a spring day or in the red fire of a long winter's evening. Some of us let those great dreams die, but others nourish and protect them, nurse them through the bad days till they bring them to the sunshine and light which comes always to those who sincerely hope that their dreams will come true." – Woodrow Wilson

All great leaders are great dreamers—they have the capacity to see what might be, and they noodle, think, and ponder about what their organizations can and will be far into the future. In today's business lexicon, we would say that they are visionary leaders.

But what separates these great dreamers from common daydreamers? Excellent leaders take those vivid, compelling, exciting dreams, and reinforce them with specific plans and goals; then they take the actions that are necessary to make their dreams become real.

"Whatever you can do, or dream you can... begin it; boldness has genius, power, and magic in it."
– Johann Wolfgang von Goethe

In working with hundreds of organizations— from three-person startups to the top management teams of multinational corporations—I find, time and time again, that one of the most common problems facing most ailing organizations is lack of a clearly-defined vision. When people don't really know where they are going, they find themselves wandering all over the place—wasting time, opportunity, talent, and resources.

One of my tests to see if a company has a clearly-defined vision is to walk through its offices and ask 20 or 30 employees at random—from front-line workers all the way to senior managers—to describe for me, in as much detail as possible, what their company will look like in three to five years. In most companies, people look at me like

I'm from another planet: "Ha ha, you are so funny, Mr. Consultant Man!" Then people rush back to work on some project, with no idea why they are doing it—knowing only that it needs to get done right away.

I have to laugh, just so I won't cry.

In contrast—when I ask the same question in the great organizations I've worked with—the answers I hear may not all be exactly the same, but they do reflect a common vision. The employees have similar ideas about what they are trying to achieve, where they are all going together, why it is important, and why they are committed to making it happen. Such similarity is a sign that a visionary leader has successfully communicated a clear, vivid, and compelling picture of the future, a vision to which the entire team is passionately committed.

"The man without a purpose is like a ship without a rudder – a waif, a nothing, a no man."
– Thomas Carlyle

"It is a poor and disgraceful thing not to be able to reply, with some degree of certainty, to the simple questions, 'What will you be? What will you do?'"
– *John Foster*

"Either control your own destiny, or someone else will."
– *Jack Welch*

We've all heard sayings like these so often they've become clichés, yet you have to admit that they're absolutely correct. To reach greatness in business—or in anything, for that matter— you must have a very clear idea of what you want to achieve. If you want to win the race, you must be able to show people exactly where the finish line is. This is the job of the leader—to point the way. Once you have developed a vivid and exciting picture of what sort of future you want to create, it is a relatively straightforward process to determine the necessary steps you must take to get there.

Let's Make It Simple

You need to have a clear idea of what you want to achieve. This is such a fundamental yet profound idea that my partners and I struggled to develop different ways to teach it to business owners and leaders in a style that they would remember and apply. What we finally created was a sort of mathematical equation that focuses on key elements and the importance of vision. I should warn you that this only looks like a math equation—if you plug in real numbers, it won't work, but for explaining vision, it's perfect. The key elements are:

$$D = \frac{IO}{Op}$$

D = Decision

IO = Intended Outcome

Op = Options

Before I explain the equation, let me give you an example.

Let's say I'm visiting a friend in Chicago and casually mention to him, "David, I'm getting pretty hungry. Could you suggest somewhere to go for dinner?"

If that's all the information I give, David is going to have a hard time picking exactly the right place for me. Given the way I've phrased my question, there are thousands of restaurants in Chicago that might meet my dining needs. Because I have given almost no description of my Intended Outcome for dining, I am faced with the prospect of thousands of possible Options. My vague question makes it extremely difficult, if not impossible, for David to make a successful suggestion.

If I say, however, "David, I'm getting pretty hungry. Could you recommend a really good Mexican restaurant, one that serves those jumbo margaritas and has fresh homemade salsa? I don't want to have to wait more than 10 minutes to get seated, and I don't want to drive more than 15 minutes to get there. I'd like the meals to be under $25, and I hate places that are loud and smoky."

I've now given a much clearer and more specific Intended Outcome for my desired dining experience. Presented with this new, detailed information, David is probably left with very few acceptable suggestions. He might know of only two or three restaurants that meet these highly specific and measurable criteria. Rephrasing my question has enabled us to shift from thousands of options and a difficult, confusing decision to only a few acceptable options and a much clearer, simpler decision.

To put this example into the language of leadership: When people in an organization do not have a clear, detailed, and specific vision of where they are trying to go, they become overwhelmed by the myriad of options and opportunities pouring in from every direction. People are scared to make decisions because they have no idea what specific outcomes they are trying to achieve. Fear, indecision, conflict, and confusion rule the day.

On the other hand, the more focused your Intended Outcome, the fewer possible acceptable Options you have so it is easier for people throughout the organization to make fast, effective decisions.

A clear and specific vision is the foundation of empowerment, delegation, and teamwork. A vivid and compelling vision is what motivates people to act. A focused and measurable Intended Outcome is the key element in successful teams, and must be driven by the leader.

Having a clear vision of what you want to achieve also allows you to do something extremely important—find the courage to say NO!

I see the greatest amount of stress created when people can't say no. People who join five committees, take on three new projects, volunteer in the community, and try to keep some balance in their lives wind up getting over-extended, rushed, stressed, and angry.

I had an experience that really demonstrated to me the importance of being able to say no. I was facilitating a special workshop for the top campus leaders at the University of Delaware; we were discussing how important it is to learn to say no in order to focus on the important things in their

24

lives, when suddenly a young woman in the corner of the room began to cry loudly. I was afraid that I had said something to upset her, and asked what was wrong.

She looked up, tears streaming from her eyes, and said, "All my life I've wanted to be a lawyer. I came to this university and studied hard and have good grades, but last weekend I was taking the LSATS (the entrance exams for law school), and fell asleep in the middle of them and failed. The reason I fell asleep is because I'd been up all night long the three nights before the exam, building my sorority's homecoming float, because nobody else would work on it and they asked me to finish it."

She began to sob almost uncontrollably as she finished, "I wonder how I'll feel in five years when I know that I may have thrown my entire career away, just because I couldn't say no."

Unfortunately, I hear the same kinds of stories in corporations across the country—stories about people who are doing things they don't enjoy, with people they don't like, that add no value to their organizations or lives—only to look up and realize that whole years have slipped by.

A Clear Vision Gives Your Efforts Focus

When you know exactly what you *should* be doing, it's much easier to decide what you *should not* be doing. Knowing your intended outcome will help you and the people on your team say no to anything that will not directly help you achieve your goals.

Experts on the subject will tell you that there is no such thing as *time management*—this is actually a matter of *priority management*. Do the things that are important to you; say no to the distractions and the trivial. This *does not* mean that you can immediately quit everything you don't want to be doing. It might take a while to extricate yourself from some of your commitments, but if, day by day, you learn to focus on what is most important and say no to what is not, eventually you will have shaken free from the shackles of time wasters and activities that add no value to your work or your life. To reach that point, you must first identify what is really important.

"This is the true joy in life, the being used for a purpose recognized by yourself as a mighty one; the being thoroughly worn out before you are thrown on the scrap heap; the being a force of nature instead of a feverish, selfish little clod of ailments and grievances complaining that the world will not devote itself to making you happy." – George Bernard Shaw

How Do You Create a Business or Personal Vision?

Even though I've helped more than 80 organizations create vision statements, I don't believe there are any hard and fast rules for how you must go about that process. The goal is simply to create a detailed, vivid, compelling, and clear picture of what you want the future to look like. You may involve a lot of people—a very good idea in an organization—or you may work alone. The process could take you just a few hours, or up to several months.

A word of caution: Don't try to make your vision so completely detailed, so incredibly exhaustive, and so perfect that it never gets completed. Do the best you possibly can with the information you have available, then get on with the job of making your vision real.

Creating a vision is simply a process of asking and answering a series of important questions. The first and most important question that excellent leaders ask before they attempt to develop a meaningful and effective vision, either for themselves or their organization, is: "What are the core values on which this vision will be based?" Without a strong commitment to some key fundamental values, there can be no long-lasting success.

Personal and Business Values

Determining your core personal and business values—describing them fully—and then working hard every day to put those values into practice is one of the most profound tasks of your life as a leader. These values are the touchstones, the guiding principles that leaders use in every decision they make, every action they take, and in all their interactions with family, friends, and business associates. When you have clear values, you create the focus required to make the sound, consistent decisions every great leader must make.

"A man's true greatness lies in the consciousness of an honest purpose in life, founded on a just estimate of himself and everything else, on frequent self-examinations, and a steady obedience to the rule which he knows to be right, without troubling himself with what others might think or say, or whether they do or do not do that which he thinks and says." – Marcus Aurelius

It is surprising how few people have taken the

time to identify the core values by which they aspire to live their lives or run their organizations. I have conducted thousands of surveys at my seminars, where I always ask: "On a scale of 1 to 10—where 1 is not at all important and 10 is extremely important—how important do you believe it is to live a values-based life?" The average score is 9.87, the highest rating of any question I ask. (For those of you who don't know statistics, 9.87 is an insanely high average.)

Later in the survey, I ask, "Do you currently have a written list of the personal core values that you use to guide your life on a daily basis?" The answer is shocking: 98 percent DO NOT!

Living a values-based life is ranked as the most important thing in the survey, yet only two people in 100 have ever taken the time to sit down and really think in earnest about the specific values that will guide their lives. I've heard many times that most people spend more time planning vacations than they do planning their own lives—sadly, my experience confirms that fact.

I urge you to take the time for a serious exploration of which core values you want to drive your life and the organizations you will lead. Your personal values are perhaps the most crucial elements in your success—or your failure—as a leader.

Plans and Goals

"Observing the lives of people who have mastered adversity, I have repeatedly noted that they have defined their visions, established their goals, and irrespective of obstacles, committed themselves to their achievement." – Ari Kiev

"Before everything else, getting ready is the secret to success." – Henry Ford

As I mentioned in the first paragraph of this chapter, the thing that separates visionary leaders from simple daydreamers is that leaders reinforce their ideas with solid plans and goals.

Planning and goal setting, especially for a large business, can become extremely complicated if you let these tasks get out of control. I have worked with clients who proudly showed me their 300-plus-page strategic plan—after they took 30 minutes to find it and wipe the dust off the cover. In most such cases, the majority of time, effort, and money go into creating the massive document, while very little of these same resources go into implementing the plan—exactly the opposite of how the plan should be created and used.

Good plans are simple, straightforward, and action-oriented. An effective plan has three core elements—a baseline, a vision, and an action plan.

A baseline is an honest and thorough assessment of your organization based on key indicators such as revenues, sales, re-work, safety, quality, product lines, market share, customer service scores, membership, fundraising, etc. The measures you choose will depend on your industry and your unique organization. The most common tool used for this task is called a S.W.O.T. analysis, an in-depth and unflinchingly honest examination of your organization's internal Strengths and Weaknesses coupled with external Opportunities and Threats that might affect you.

A vision is the vivid, compelling, detailed description of where you are trying to take the organization, focused on the same key measurements used in the Baseline.

An action plan is a step-by-step set of plans and quantifiable goals that will move the organization from where it is today to the future you have envisioned.

"An intelligent plan is the first step to success. The man who plans knows where he is going, knows what progress he is making, and has a pretty good idea when he will arrive. Planning is the open road to your destination. If you don't know where you are going, how can you expect to get there?" – Basil S. Walsh

"I will prepare and some day my chance will come."
– Abraham Lincoln

Although there are many ways to approach goal setting, I believe the SMART model is one of the best. All of your goals—both business and personal—should meet the following criteria.

S = SPECIFIC. Make your goal as clear, detailed, and unambiguous as possible. Write your goal out in as much detail as you can—not just in a few hastily jotted bullet points, but in whole paragraphs. The more detail in which you can describe the goal, the easier it is to discover what you will have to do to reach it. You may later condense your goal to a set of key ideas, but make sure to begin with a complete and thorough examination of each of your goals, including why they are important to you and what you will need to do to achieve them.

M = MEASURABLE. You must be able to measure your progress towards attainment of the goal—the number of pounds you want to lose, the amount of product you want to sell, the GPA you want to achieve, the bonus you want to earn, the percentage of market share you want to capture. You need specific numbers and percentages to give you a very clear idea of your desired results.

A = AGREED UPON. Be sure that everyone involved in working toward the goal agrees to give this task 100 percent of their efforts. The more people you have on your team working with you to achieve the goal, the higher your chances of success. Conversely, if the people around you do not support your goal, it will be very difficult to make any positive progress. If you are in a team setting, make sure that each goal is assigned to a specific person who will be held accountable for its attainment. A goal with no owner will not be reached by itself!

R = REALISTIC. Set your goals high, but not so high that they are unattainable. Here is an example: You decided your goal to lose 20 pounds... this month! You can definitely lose 20 pounds, but not in 30 days; it's unrealistic. So on the 17th of the month when you've only lost five pounds (which is actually fantastic), you have only 14 days left to lose 15 pounds. You realize that reaching your goal is hopeless. Since you'll never be able to make it, you go directly to the grocery store to drown your failure in a gallon of double-chunk chocolate death. You put all the pounds you've lost back on, and add a few new ones.

I have seen similar scenarios happen in a number of client companies. Companies set a completely unrealistic goal, such as doubling sales in six months. Four months into the project, sales have only increased by 20 percent (actually quite impressive), and everyone realizes that they will not be able to make the 100 percent increase goal with just 60 days left—so they give up, and sales fall off dramatically. The result? Sales end up the same as or worse than they were before the goal was set.

You need to set goals that will challenge you, but also goals that you can realistically achieve.

T = TIME BOUND. Put a specific date on each step of the process, so that you can measure progress and keep the plan on track. A goal without a due date is just a wish.

"Failing to plan is planning to fail." – Anonymous

Action

Another critical element that distinguishes great leaders is the massive amount of action they apply to their plan, once it has been established.

"Leadership is action, not position." – Gerald Greenwald

"Even if you're on the right track, you'll get run over if you just sit there." – Will Rogers

"The ordinary man is involved in action, the hero acts." – Henry Miller

I have a handful of what I call "consultant guru phrases" that I find myself repeating constantly. One key phrase is "execute to plan." You can have the most exciting vision imaginable. You can create a fantastic plan that is measurable, time bound, and all those great things. Your plan will be completely useless, however, if you don't get up every morning and make it happen.

This point was dramatically highlighted for me

in a meeting with the Chief Financial Officer of a $700 million United States-based company that had just been purchased by $6 billion Japanese conglomerate. The CFO told me that the only reason his new parent company was more than eight times larger than his old company was that the new parent company actually followed its strategic plan.

"We take the brightest people in our organization and go off site for two weeks to build a very sophisticated and expensive strategic plan; then we put it on the shelf and don't look at it for another year," he said. "They actually carry theirs around to every meeting and use it on a daily basis."

You must infuse your organization with what I call a culture of urgency—make it a place where fast action is rewarded, and people do whatever it takes to make the business plan a business reality.

"Think like a man of action, act like a man of thought."
– Henry-Louis Bergson

Excellence...by Design

In 1999, at the age of 34, I made a decision that has had a strong positive impact on my life—I joined a fraternity! I'd decided not to go Greek in college, but as I began to lecture on leadership at universities around the country, I was asked by a number of organizations if I would consider becoming an alumni initiate. After careful research and serious thought, I joined Pi Kappa Phi, an organization dedicated to becoming America's leading fraternity by "Building Better Men" through a strong, values-based leadership culture and the core ideal of service above self.

Each year, Pi Kappa Phi holds a series of leadership schools and conferences where almost 1,000 of this country's brightest young men come to learn how to be better students, leaders, and citizens. It was for one such event that I was asked to present a special keynote address on the theme of excellence by design, which became the genesis of this book and the foundation of one of the most important concepts I teach.

Because I take my role as an educator very seriously, I spent almost eight weeks preparing for what became a 15-minute speech. I reviewed every book I had on leadership and excellence; I called dozens of CEOs and company presidents; and I had four college interns doing research, all in an effort to understand better, "What is excellence and how do you achieve it?"

In the end, I was able to condense all the information we collected to three key qualities that I call the touchstones of excellence. To achieve excellence in school, in business, or in life, you must have focus, discipline, and action.

FOCUS. You must have a clear idea of exactly what excellence means to you, and stay focused on that ideal.

You'll need to develop a values-based personal philosophy of excellence that permeates every aspect of your life. You'll need to spend a good deal of time in serious thought about what is truly important to you, what you value the most in your life, the kind of person you really want to become, and the legacy you want to leave in this world, both as an individual and as a leader of others.

In all of my research of the greatest leaders throughout history, the development of a personal philosophy of life—and an incredibly intense focus on exemplifying that philosophy—is a constant.

"The person who makes a success of living is the one who seeks his goal steadily and aims for it unswervingly." – Cecil B. DeMille

DISCIPLINE. You must have enough personal discipline to live true to your philosophy of excellence, even when the circumstances and people around you make it difficult.

Maintaining a high level of self-discipline that is centered on your personal philosophy of excellence is perhaps the most difficult prescription in this book. Other people will try to hold you back. Situations will seem hopeless. You will be

41

challenged to choose an easier path. People who achieve greatness do so, however, because they have the desire and discipline to do things that average people are unwilling to do!

"The difference between a successful person and others is not a lack of strength, not a lack of knowledge, but rather a lack of will." – Vince Lombardi

"We are what we repeatedly do." – Aristotle

ACTION. You must take action to achieve excellence.

The level of excellence you achieve is directly proportional to the amount of effort you apply. Simply talk about excellence, and you'll get nothing. Act on excellence—every day, in everything you do—and you will achieve it.

"All men seek one goal: success or happiness. The only way to achieve true success is to express yourself completely in service to society. First have a definite, clear, practical idea—a goal, an objective. Second, have

the necessary means to achieve your ends—wisdom, money, materials, and methods. Third, adjust all your means to that end." – Aristotle

Looking for some great examples of achieving excellence? Let's consider Olympic gold medalists, the best athletes in the world at what they do. How many sports do they participate in? One. How much discipline do they exhibit? Constant. How much effort do they expend? Superhuman. To prove their excellence, these athletes will work out six to eight hours every day, year after year after year—all for one brief event that lasts perhaps 10 seconds.

Intense Focus + Incredible Discipline x Massive Action = Best in the World!

Olympic medalists are inspiring examples of people striving for excellence. Let me caution you with an important note, however. Contrary to what many of us have been taught, we don't all have to achieve the Olympic level of excellence. The price that must be paid to ascend to Olympic levels of expertise and achievement is extreme. When I really push people hard to get them to tell themselves the truth, very few people honestly aspire to be the best in the world at what they do. Most people simply want to have a moderate level of professional success, while still maintaining a normal and happy life. It is much more reasonable, and I strongly encourage you, to design your personal philosophy of excellence on a foundation of balance.

Set high standards and expectations in your leadership role, to be sure; but balance these standards and expectations with excellence in family, community, service, and fun. It is entirely possible to be truly excellent and still have time to go to the gym, enjoy dinner at home, and spend weekends with your friends!

Key Points

» Have a clear, vivid, compelling vision of where you want to go, both in your organization and in your life!

» Be an evangelist for the vision throughout your organization. Talk about it all the time—in meetings, at lunch, in the newsletter, by email, in every way possible. Keep the vision out in front of people to help them to see where they are going at all times.

» Create a set of SMART goals—a specific, measurable, agreed-upon, realistic plan and timeline to achieve that vision.

» Use the vision and plan to foster empowerment. Tell people where you are going and show them how to get there. Then, let them make the vision real.

» Execute to plan. The amount of success you will achieve will be directly proportional to the amount of focused effort you apply to the vision and the plan.

» Create a culture of urgency throughout your organization.

» Focus + Discipline x Action =
EXCELLENCE BY DESIGN

"You can't build a reputation on what you are going to do." – Henry Ford

2
Opportunity Is Everywhere

"All you get in this world is opportunity, the rest is up to you. Don't expect life to be fair, because it will not always be, but it will respond to your willingness to work very, very hard to turn opportunity into success."
– *Thomas A. Carvel*

Excellent leaders believe in opportunity. As the noted author Stephen Covey might say, "They have an abundance mentality, not a scarcity mentality." Regardless of age, race, gender, education, financial standing, or religious beliefs, excellent leaders focus on possibilities, not problems.

Many of the leaders I have met and studied had to overcome enormous odds to become successful, yet few—if any—ever dwelt on those difficulties. Yes, these leaders were often at a disadvantage; yes, people treated them poorly; yes, they had to work harder than other people to get the same results; yes, these things were unfair, but since these leaders never expected life to be fair, they simply figured out what it would take to become successful—and did it. They didn't blame others, or make excuses, but instead took responsibility for their own futures and focused on finding ways to make positive things happen. You will have to do these things, too.

"Opportunities do not come with their value stamped upon them. Everyone must be challenged. A day dawns, quiet like other days; in it a single hour comes, quite like other hours; but in that day and in that hour the chance of a lifetime faces us. To face every opportunity of life thoughtfully and ask its meaning bravely and earnestly, is the only way to meet the supreme opportunities when they come."
– Maltbie Babcock.

Creating opportunity is perhaps the most difficult and subtle of the characteristics I am sharing with you in this book, because creating opportunity has an almost mystical quality about it. Because great leaders have a powerful belief in boundless opportunity, and because they dedicate their lives to looking for opportunity, I assert that they actually *create* many of the opportunities in their lives.

"The world has a way of giving what is demanded of it. If you are frightened and look for failure and poverty, you will get them, no matter how hard you try to succeed. Lack of faith in yourself, in what life will do for you, cuts you off from the good things of the world. Expect victory and you make victory. Nowhere is this truer than in business life, where bravery and faith bring both material and spiritual rewards."
– Preston Bradley

There is a good deal of scientific research to support the idea that you create your own opportunities. One of the main ways human beings do this is through a phenomenon called the Reticular Activating System (RAS).

Basically, the RAS is a type of mental radar that focuses your attention and sensory perceptions on whatever target your mind chooses. The best way to demonstrate this is with a classic example. You

49

decide it's time to buy a new car, so you go down to the local dealer to take a look around. While walking across the lot, you spy a hot new red convertible. Wow, what a car! You've never seen one quite like it. You picture yourself behind the wheel; all your friends will be jealous because you own the only car like it in the whole town! You simply must have this car.

You tell the salesman you are interested and go into the showroom to talk numbers. The talk does not go the way you had hoped; the car is well out of your price range. You want the car badly, but you really don't think you can afford it, so you tell the salesman you'll need to go home and think about it for a day or two. He reluctantly lets you leave the lot.

Now, driving home and thinking of this hot red convertible, what do you suddenly start to see all over the place? Yep—that exact car. There is one parked in a driveway, here comes one in the other lane, there's another in the drive-through. What happened? Did God suddenly populate the streets with this car? Did red convertibles appear from nowhere? No, the cars were there all along—you simply didn't see them. But now that you are thinking about red cars, focusing on them—they are everywhere.

Seeing opportunity works exactly the same way. When you focus on potential opportunity—when it is always at the front of your mind, always in your thoughts—your Reticular Activating System is constantly searching, looking, trying to find anything that even resembles an opportunity. This is why it is so important as a leader to have a vivid vision and specific written goals—to give yourself an extremely clear picture of what you want to achieve, so your brain knows what to search for. And, believe me—your brain will find it.

So why didn't you see any of those red cars on the way to the dealership? The answer is because you were NOT focusing on them, and that lack of focus actually made them invisible to you!

This is a critical point: *You become what you fo-*

cus on in your life, and are blind to the things that are outside your focus. If you are not focused on opportunity, it will pass you by all day long. You will walk right past chances to achieve your goals, meet new people, help your team, get involved in exciting projects, and change your life.

One of your most important tasks as a leader is to create and sustain a positive focus for yourself and the people you lead.

"When you want a thing deeply, earnestly, and intensely, this feeling of desire reinforces your will and arouses in you the determination to work for the desired object. When you have a distinct purpose in view, your work becomes of absorbing interest. You bend your best powers to it; you give it concentrated attention; you think of little else than the realization of this purpose; your will is stimulated into unusual activity, and as a consequence you do your work with an increasing sense of power."– Grenville Kleiser

The idea that what you become as a person is inextricably linked to what you choose as the focus of your mind is one of the most profound concepts I have ever encountered. Once I understood the ramifications of incorporating this idea into my life and business, it completely changed the way I viewed the world. This concept can be difficult to grasp, but once you think about it long enough and achieve a deep level of understanding, it can actually change your life.

There is another scientific concept related to this idea that you might find interesting. In 1927, the famous Danish physicist Neils Bohr created what he called the Principle of Complementarity. According to Bohr, light has the ability to demonstrate simultaneously both wave-like and particle-like properties! This phenomenon occurs because our perception of the behavior of light is completely dependent upon the tools we use to examine it.

If we examine a light photon with a particle detector, we see it as a particle. If we examine a light photon with a wave detector, we see it as a wave. Neither measurement is more real or accurate than the other—they are both correct. At any one moment, we are able to observe either a wave or a particle—yet both descriptions are required to fully define the attributes of light. The properties of light become whatever you choose to focus on!

"The path comes into existence only when we observe it."
– Werner Heisenberg

What does this idea mean to you and me in the real world? I will make my point with a simple but powerful illustration. Take a look at the shape below; is that shape convex or concave?

)

Some will say convex, and some will say concave. The truth is, both views are correct! It is concave, and it is convex, but—here is the point—**it cannot be both at the same time!**

If you place the center of your focus to the left

of the shape, it will appear concave; if you place the center of your focus to the right, it will appear convex. Depending on where you focus, you create the ultimate reality of the object. And because the object can only have one shape at a time, when you focus on its having one shape, the other shape becomes invisible to you. For the moment, the alternate shape ceases to exist.

Put another way, the object has the potential to be either concave or convex, but it is neither until you look at it. Once you observe it, though, you make a decision in your mind about which shape it is—and, in that instant, it becomes either convex or concave for you.

Please note that this also means that the people sitting next to you might see the same object in the opposite way—and that they are just as right in their interpretation as you are in yours. Opposite, yet right—think about that and how it applies in your life and organization!

Does this mean that you are creating your reality from moment to moment by the choices and distinctions you make about the people and objects around you? I believe that it does. I believe you play a very large part in creating the world you live in, by the way in which you decide to view it.

"We do not see things as they are, we see things as we are." – Talmudic Saying

"What the future holds for us depends on what we hold for the future."– William E. Holler

"What we see depends mainly on what we look for." – John Lubbock

"Every man carries with him the world in which he must live." – F. Marion Crawford

If you focus on failure, loss, anger, or obstacles, that is what you and the people you lead will see. If you focus on opportunity, success, fun, and happiness, then that is what you will create. Excellent leaders focus on opportunity—and help others around them to focus on it as well—and thereby see opportunity everywhere.

"You are today where your thoughts have brought you. You cannot escape the result of your thoughts, but you can endure and learn, can accept and be glad. You will realize the vision (not the idle wish) of your heart, be it base or beautiful, or a mixture of both, for you will always gravitate toward that which you, secretly, most love. Into your hands will be placed the exact results of your thoughts; you will receive that which you earn; no more, no less. Whatever your present environment may be, you will fall, remain or rise with your thoughts, your vision, your ideal. You will become as small as your controlling desire; as great as your dominant aspiration." – James Allan

Key Points

» Life is not fair. It was never supposed to be, and it never will be.

» Regardless of challenges, opportunity for success is everywhere.

» You become what you focus on, so focus intently on finding opportunity, success, happiness and joy everywhere you look—and that is what you will find.

» The world is not as we see it, but as we *choose* to see it. Change your focus, and you can literally change your life.

» Help other people change their focus, and you can help them change their lives.

"What helps luck is a habit of watching for opportunities, of having a patient, but restless mind, of sacrificing one's ease or vanity, of uniting love of detail to foresight and of passing through hard times bravely and cheerfully." – Victor Cherbuliez

3
Embrace Risk

"Risk! Risk anything! Care no more for the opinion of others, for those voices. Do the hardest thing on earth for you. Act for yourself. Face the truth."
– Katherine Mansfield

"The greatest mistake in life is to be continually fearing that you will make one." – Elbert Hubbard

By its very definition, leadership is about being a catalyst for change, and change inherently involves risk. Even a passing review of the lives of excellent leaders is a study in bold attempts, daring tries, extravagant experiments, and sometimes even devastating setbacks. Leaders understand that in the effort to be great, there also lies the possibility of great failure. But they embrace that risk and use it as a driving force in accomplishing their dreams and goals. Far from taking foolish risks, great leaders take precautions, explore options, and look at all possible outcomes; then they take seemingly audacious, but always calculated, risks.

"Homer, Socrates, Plato, Joan of Arc, Confucius, Lao-Tzu, Christ, Samuel Johnson, William and Henry James, Abraham Lincoln, Thomas Edison, Ralph Waldo Emerson, Henry David Thoreau, Thomas Jefferson, Emily Dickinson, Rainer Maria Rilke, Shakespeare, Thackeray. The list is incomplete; yet any name you add will be someone who had strength of will. These people weren't afraid. We quickly forget the cowards; we celebrate the courageous. These men and women were fighters whose clear choices lent them focus and vision. They were strong."
– Alexandra Stoddard

"In the end, it is important to remember that we cannot become what we need to be by remaining what we are." – Max De Pree

Leaders are agents for change. The leader's job is to push for new and exciting levels of achievement. For many people, that push can be very scary. Change means moving out of your precious safety zones, trying new things, and encountering the very real chance of failure. So to truly excel as a leader, you must become comfortable with taking risks and helping others to do the same.

But how do you do that? Here are two tools to help you become a more confident and successful risk taker.

1. The KSA Process

"The elimination of chance becomes an indispensable condition of man's supremacy." – René Descartes

When we examine them more closely, we find that great leaders are not really risk takers—they are actually excellent risk minimizers. To help reduce risk as much as possible, excellent leaders use what I call the KSA Process, a quick and effective way to examine, minimize, and embrace risk with confidence.

K = KNOWLEDGE

"Chance favors the prepared mind." – Louis Pasteur

The first step towards minimizing risk is to acquire knowledge. Gather as much relevant data as you reasonably can in an acceptable time frame. If you have to make a decision right away, then you'll only be able to look at readily available information. If you have more time, you can systematically search for more data needed to make a sound decision.

A recent research project studied the difference between people who failed terribly when faced with a challenging problem, as opposed to people who succeeded at a high level. The study showed that the people who failed waited until things were really bad—almost disasters—before they asked for help, and had only a few people to whom they could go to for assistance. Help came too little, too late.

The people who succeeded in the face of adversity, however, were quick to seek out help at the very first sign of trouble, and had a large network of associates and mentors who could offer them advice and information.

So here is a key leadership point: **Outstanding leaders ask for help.** They surround themselves with as many bright, talented people as possible, and go to them often for insight and assistance.

The goal, then, is to get all of the relevant information you need to make a good decision from lots of different sources, without falling into the trap of paralysis by analysis—where you spend all of your time and effort collecting information, and never get to the point of making a decision.

S = STRATEGY

The next step is to develop a strategy for going forward, while at the same time reducing your exposure to risk. Look at all the information you have amassed to determine what your realistic options are, and what the possible outcome of each decision might be. Then, create a strategy based on the best available options. Look at the data objectively, and force yourself to answer some tough but necessary "If...then..." and "What if...?" questions about yourself and your organization.

The key to success here is brutal honesty. It is easy to ask questions like, "Will we invest the additional revenue generated, or will we distribute it as profits?" True leaders must also ask the questions to which they don't really want to hear the answers, for example: "What if this strategy were to fail and cause our company to go out of business?" "How would we handle a strike at one of our supplier companies?" "What will we do if this causes people to stop sending in donations, or even quit our organization?"

It is only by exploring these worst-case scenarios and developing strategies you can live with, should these scenarios occur, that you gain the confidence to embrace big risks and make bold decisions that create positive change.

Not being willing to face tough questions is one of the greatest weaknesses I have seen in people and organizations, but pretending these questions don't exist will not make them go away.

Occasionally, the information you gather will make the best possible option seem obvious. Some of the best counsel I can offer, however, is to take an additional moment or two to look for the second right answer. I've told you not to get bogged down in endless analysis, yet it is just as important not to rush headlong into a decision using the very first idea that occurs to you or your team. There is rarely, if ever, only one right answer. Look just a little longer. The majority of the time, your first instinct will be the right one—but you may be surprised at what you discover with just five more minutes of thoughtful exploration.

A = ACTION

Once you have chosen a sound strategy, move on to the final and most critical step—taking action. Leaders know that the best strategy in the world is completely useless if they don't take action. Remember: execute to plan.

"The most effective way to deal with fear or anxiety is through the acquisition of information and through the focusing of activity." – Ari Kiev

"Business is dependent on action. It cannot go forward by hesitation. Those in executive positions must fortify themselves with facts and accept responsibility for decisions based on them. Often greater risk is involved in postponement than in making wrong decisions." – Harry A. Hopf

Excellent leaders have a clear focus (vision); they gather the best information available (from all possible sources); they use that knowledge to create a solid strategy (goals and plans); and then they create amazing success by taking action.

2. Expand Your SAS

Several years ago, I ran across an interesting concept called the Subjective Units of Discomfort Scale or SUDS, a diagnostic tool used to analyze a person's relative level of fear, anxiety, or stress regarding a specific activity or situation. Although

I heard just a brief explanation, I thought about the scale for months.

After a lot of mental gymnastics, I developed my specially customized version, which I call the Spence Anxiety Scale or SAS.

0-10 Basically asleep – no fear, anxiety or stress

11-20 Passive action – no stress

21-30 Simply engaged in a task – mild levels of stress (positive or negative)

31-40 Excited about a task – feelings of positive stress (motivation, enjoyment)

41-50 Totally absorbed in a task – high levels of positive stress (what some call "flow")

51-60 Discomfort – negative feelings of uneasiness / fear / anxiety / stress

61-70 Fight or flight response – high levels of fear / anxiety / overwhelming stress

71-80 Physiological shutdown – very high levels of fear / anxiety / debilitating stress

80+ Psychosis / death – extreme levels of fear / anxiety / toxic stress

In the early stages of the SAS, you feel little or no stress. You might be sitting around the house, watching a calming TV program, listening to soothing music, or talking on the phone with a friend. A little higher on the scale—say into the high 20s and 30s—you start to feel a little stress, but this is positive. You are becoming engaged and excited about what you are doing, so you experience a low level of fear of not performing well or having to stop the enjoyable task.

The 40-50 range is a state of very positive feelings, where you become so completely absorbed in what you are doing that you lose all sense of the passage of time, and experience peak performance or what some people call a flow state. Flow is Michael Jordan flying through the air with his tongue sticking out, or the painter who stands at the canvas for hours, forgetting to stop for lunch or to go to the bathroom.

Each of us has one or more activities that allow us to enter peak states—usually while engaged in our hobbies, but, if we are lucky, in our jobs! The goal is to engage in as many activities as possible that move us toward the 40-50 range.

"It is not work if you love what you are doing."
– Malcolm Forbes

As you move past the peak state, you head into zones of negative stress, where fear and anxiety become debilitating. Here is where the trouble starts.

In the 50-60 range, you start to have physical reactions—quickening of the pulse, increased heart rate, and shortness of breath. As you move to even higher levels, your body starts to respond more strongly. At 60-70, it is time for battle or retreat with the fight or flight syndrome; blood is sent to the major muscle groups, preparing the body for action.

At still higher levels, there may be complete loss of control as your body freezes up; this happens when people are overwhelmed by tremendous fear and anxiety. Stress beyond this point carries the risk permanent physical and mental damage, or even death.

What This Means to You

"Security is mostly a superstition. It does not exist in nature, nor do the children of men as a whole experience it. Avoiding danger is no safer in the long run than outright exposure. Life is either a daring adventure, or nothing." – Helen Keller

"The first step to turn fear into power is to accept full responsibility for your choices, behavior, and the reality of what you now have in your life. The second step is to have the courage to acknowledge and examine your fears." – James Mapes

It is extremely important to remember that the SAS is all relative to a person's individual feelings, background, emotions, and expectations. For example, many people would rate the prospect of having to get up and make a two-hour presentation to a group of 500 strangers and peers as a 60+ activity—a very high level of fear. For me, however, this is a joyful experience—I love it, so it is a 45 for me. On the other hand, the sight of blood or seeing someone in pain is a 70 for me, yet it might represent just a typical event (20-30) for most doctors and nurses.

Never assume that because something is easy and low stress for you, that it will be easy and low stress for everyone; the same event might terrify one of your team members.

Here is the point. For some people, taking *any* chances, trying new things, attempting even minimal change, is a 60+ proposition; it simply represents too much risk. As a leader, however, you must personally achieve some level of comfort with taking risks, while at the same time helping those you lead to embrace risk and change without being overwhelmed by fear or anxiety. To accomplish this feat, you'll need to help your team take the things that are now 50s, 60s, and 70s, and push them back towards a more comfortable range on the SAS. You help your team by showing people it is possible to face your fear, accept it, and overcome it.

71

"You will never stub your toe standing still. The faster you go, the more chance there is of stubbing your toe, but the more chance you have of getting somewhere."
– *Charles F. Kettering*

I'll illustrate this point with a brief personal example. Recently, I was involved with a project that seemed overwhelming to me. The personal and professional risks were very high, and I was not sure I was up to the challenge. My solution was to shock my SAS. I decided to do something I had always wanted to do, but that was probably the scariest and riskiest thing I could think of—skydiving! The thought of jumping out of a perfectly good airplane at 13,000 feet sounded extremely exciting, but also terrified me.

I can tell you with all honesty, when they opened the door to that airplane and I stepped out to the edge, I was at a full-blown 80 on the SAS. I froze. I was scared stiff—I couldn't think—I couldn't move—I was petrified. Below me, houses were the size of the type on this page. I could cover up an entire city block with my thumb. Cars were so small they looked like tiny multicolored amoebas darting around under a microscope.

And then I jumped. At first I couldn't breathe. My mind was spinning faster than I was falling. I was dizzy and dazed, dumfounded and confused—then, suddenly, I was FLYING.

It was the most awesome experience of my life, a thrill unmatched by any other—an entirely new level of fun, excitement, and joy!

When I landed safely just a few minutes later, I was more pumped and confident than I had ever been before. I thought to myself, "That was great, that was fun—and I really didn't think I could do it, because I was too scared."

The jump became a new personal SAS benchmark for me. What was previously a 78 on my personal scale was now a 52! I said to myself, "If I can do that, what else can I accomplish that I used to be afraid of—that might actually be just as much fun?"

That is a very powerful question to ask yourself!

Skydiving is an extreme example, and I'm in no way suggesting that you have to jump out of a plane or walk on fire to improve your leadership skills. Rather, I am saying that you must stretch yourself to become more comfortable and confident in your ability to take acceptable risks.

Try something new, make a tough decision, have that difficult discussion with someone on your team, take a stand for something. Embrace the risk. If you want to grow, if you want your team to grow, if you want your organization to grow, it is essential to recognize and accept that growth demands change, and change entails risk; change and risk are two sides of the same coin.

"The only security is courage."
– Francois La Rochefoucauld

The SAS can also be useful for members of your team who are having an especially difficult time dealing with the fear of taking a risk. The scale gives you a way to help these people assign an analytical number to what can be a very emotional situation. For example, let's say you ask Bob to make a presentation to one of your biggest clients. Just looking at Bob, you can tell he is in distress and has a lot of fear and anxiety, but you also know that it is difficult for Bob to discuss his feelings with you.

You can ask Bob to tell you where he ranks this assignment on the SAS, to which he replies, "Well, I'm about a 67 or so." You now know that Bob is experiencing a very high level of stress.

You can then ask him a very powerful question. "Bob, what can I do to help you move this from a 67 to a 57 or even a 47?"

Now the two of you can pick out specific actions to help Bob carry on with the project and overcome his fear. Possibly he needs some training, or special equipment, or maybe he would like you to review the presentation and help him practice it. The point is, he has overcome his fear and is moving forward with taking positive risks.

"Whenever you make a decision, whenever you act, you are never just doing, you are becoming."
– Tom Morris

When faced with a new venture, a risky project, or a big business decision, it always helps me to remember that all the great leaders throughout time had a first day on the job, too. They did not always know what to do; they were scared, nervous, and anxious at times—but they went ahead anyway.

"The history of great leaders is the history of great risk takers." – John Spence

"If all else fails, immortality can always be assured by spectacular error." – John Kenneth Galbraith

Key Points

» Great leaders have to take great risks—it is their job.

» Great leaders are actually skilled risk minimizers.

» Use KSA – Knowledge / Strategy / Action – to confront and minimize a risk.

» Use the SAS to put an analytical number on an emotional feeling, and then deal logically with how to reduce your feelings of fear and anxiety.

» As a leader, you must help your team become more comfortable with change, risk, and failure. Otherwise, your team will risk nothing, and thereby accomplish nothing.

*"Success is never final and failure is never fatal.
It is courage that counts." – George F. Tilton*

4
Believe In People

"The best leaders are those most interested in sur-rounding themselves with assistants and associates smarter than they are – being frank in admitting this – and willing to pay for such talent." – Amos Parrish

I know a secret, but no one wants to hear it. It has been my battle cry for years, but it falls on deaf ears. I have jumped up and down about it in meetings and on stages far and wide, and still they do not listen. Here it is: **You cannot have a great organization without great people.**

I know it sounds so simple that it's almost offensive, but shockingly few leaders truly understand the weight of that statement.

I have worked with countless clients who tell me they want to build world-class organizations, yet they are unwilling to do what it takes to get and keep the best people. These clients hire people haphazardly, train people very little if at all, and pay their people the absolute minimum; then they can't understand why they aren't getting the stellar results they were expecting.

"The wise man will want to be ever with him who is better than himself." – Plato

Excellent leaders believe in people; they surround themselves with the brightest, most talented and focused people they can find, then spend the majority of their time helping those people succeed. These leaders are not intimidated or jealous of their superstar subordinates—rather, they understand that the better the team they build, the farther they will go as the team's leader. As the Chairman and CEO of a $17 billion corporation remarked, "As leaders, we often tend to think we know a lot more than we really do. We forget that it's the people that are working with us that really make us what we are."

As exceptional as some of our great leaders throughout time have been, not one of them accomplished what they did by themselves. If you were to do an in-depth study of the lives of out-standing leaders—which I have done—you would find that many of their achievements were, in large part, due to the talents and actions of the people with whom they surrounded themselves.

"Associate with men of good quality if you esteem your own reputation; for it is better to be alone than in bad company."– George Washington

"Every man becomes, to a certain degree, what the people he generally converses with are." – Phillip Dormer Stanhope, Earl of Chesterfield

"Good company and good discourse are the sinews of virtue." – Izaak Walton

The Foundation

What is the foundation of all strong, positive relationships between leaders and the people they lead? What is the one thing you must have with your team if you expect them to follow you willingly?

When I ask this question in my classes around the world, the answer is always the same: TRUST.

How do you create and maintain a high level of trust as a leader? It is simple, but not easy. You start with the "Four C's."

The First Two C's = Competency and Concern

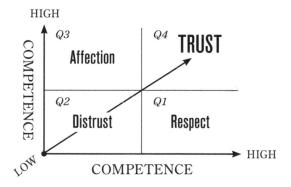

The first two C's serve as the axes of the chart, and are Competency and Concern. In other words, how well do you perform your job, and how much do you care about your people?

Q1: RESPECT

In quadrant one, we have someone who has a high degree of competency but a low degree of concern. She is a person with superior technical skills, but no people skills. She knows and performs her job extremely well, but she is a pain in the butt. The analogy I use is that of a world-famous brain surgeon with a terrible bedside manner; you'd want her to operate on you if you were ill, but you wouldn't play golf with her or have her over to the house for a barbecue.

Many would-be leaders try to command from this position, attempting to use intimidation and superior intelligence to control their people. A group will follow such a person for a while out of respect, but they will never give 100 percent of their discretionary effort and will abandon that leader quickly if the leader becomes too abusive or demanding.

Q2: DISTRUST

In the second quadrant, we have a person who is both incompetent and uncaring—a person who creates distrust. This combination of qualities represents the antithesis of a leader, yet is found too often in organizations. Good people simply will not put up with this combination in a leader; they will move on quickly. Ironically, the bad people stay!

Q3: AFFECTION

In quadrant three, we find a manager who ranks high on concern but low on competence. He is the person who tries to lead by being your best buddy. He is fun, nice, and friendly, but messes up project after project for the entire team. Once again, good people will not put up with this sort of leader for very long—it is just too frustrating. People might feel affection for such managers, but they neither respect them nor trust them to lead.

Q4: TRUST

The final quadrant represents what you aim for as an effective leader—high levels of competence in your job performance, and high levels of concern for your people. This does not mean that you are best friends with everybody and know how to do every job in the organization; it simply means that you know your own job exceptionally well, and show genuine empathy and concern for the members of your group.

I am now going to share with you the personal mantra of great leaders: **"I am good at what I do—and I do it because I care about you."**

If you live this mantra—if you work every single day to improve your skills and competence, and do this all in an effort to help your team, grow the people you work with, and show genuine concern for your followers—you will become an excellent leader.

"Until you become the sort of person that others want to follow, you are not a true leader." – John Spence

This statement is the truth, and it is powerful stuff. In order for a person to follow you willingly and give their very best efforts for you, they have to:

» Respect you – for your knowledge & competence

» Like you – because you respect them

» Believe that you care about them – both as employees and as individuals

» Believe that you will tell them the truth – all the time and every time

The Third C = Communication

The ability to communicate clearly—to create understanding between you and all your people—is perhaps the single most important leadership skill you need to develop. If you are in a position of leadership—regardless of your formal title—every word you speak, every action you take, and every decision you make are sure to be scrutinized throughout your organization. You cannot simply blurt out whatever you are thinking if you wish to maintain trust and credibility with the people you hope to influence and direct. Go back and read that entire paragraph again—I simply cannot stress strongly enough how important personal communication is to becoming a successful leader.

There is a fundamental rule of organizational communication that you need to remember: People without access to good information cannot take responsibility for their decisions ("I didn't get the memo," "Nobody told me," "I don't know anything about that.")

On the other hand, people with access to lots of good information cannot help but take responsibility for their actions. Clear and specific communication is the cornerstone of delegation, empowerment, and quick action—all key components of building a great organization.

Great leaders share as much information with their people as they legally can, in open, honest, and straightforward ways. Through multiple sources—meetings, newsletters, training, casual conversations, team gatherings, beer blasts, birthday parties, and more—great leaders are constantly focusing their entire organizations on their visions and plans, on opportunity and success.

C.C.C.T.

In the last few months, I have worked with several clients who were struggling mightily to build high-functioning teams. As I conducted intensive surveys and one-on-one interviews in all of these organizations, yet another trend emerged that I realized I had been dealing with for years.

Each of the people in these groups knew exactly what was wrong in their organizations long before I'd been hired to uncover the problems and fix them. Every person could identify the problems, and even had some good ideas about how to solve them, but for some amazing reason they were all afraid to talk to each other about their perceptions! They would mumble, complain, and moan about a team member—but they would not walk 30 feet down the hall and actually talk to the person with whom they were having difficulties. They would come up with a spectacular idea to greatly improve productivity and success—and keep it to themselves. They would go home and tell their families, friends, and neighbors about all the problems at their office—but they wouldn't say a word in meetings.

So I began teaching what I felt were some core concepts about good communication that these people were ignoring—nothing particularly earth shattering, but something these folks needed to be reminded of and held accountable for implementing. I call it: C-C-C-T.

Courage. You must have the guts, the backbone, and the courage to deal with difficult and awkward situations. These situations will not go away on their own—they must be addressed—and, as the leader, it often falls on you to deal with these uncomfortable topics. You must take full responsibility for creating good communications on your team.

Candor. Be as frank, open, and completely honest as possible, while still respecting the feelings and fears of those you lead. Tell the truth—with love.

Clarity. The only goal of communication is mutual understanding. You must keep communicating—with different approaches, styles, mediums, and techniques—until you achieve the desired outcome. It does not matter if you have to try 30 different ways—you are not communicating effectively until all parties clearly understand your message. This can be very, very hard work!

Timeliness. Talk about the subject as soon as it is prudent. Every now and then, it is a good idea to let emotion subside and let the subject rest a bit. In most cases, however, the best course of action is to address the situation immediately. Don't let problems fester; don't allow people to sit in their offices and build small concerns into huge problems. Waiting too long to talk about problems is being like the baseball coach who tells his team—after they've lost the game—that he saw them making mistakes in the first inning. Let people know right away what they need to do to fix bad situations and get things moving forward in a positive direction.

Communication is the act by which leaders create motivation and results. With sensitivity, care, and deep concern about what you say and how you say it, and what you do and what you don't do, you can build your leadership credibility while energizing and inspiring your team members to achieve higher and higher levels of success.

The Fourth C = Consistency

When I ask audiences how long it might take to build up a high level of trust by clearly demonstrating competence and concern, the answers range from a few weeks to a few years. I then ask them how long it takes to destroy that trust, and the answer is always the same: seconds.

Here is the most difficult concept for aspiring leaders to grasp: **People judge you by your actions, not your intentions. If you want to be an outstanding leader, you must be a living example of what you are asking your followers to be. Period.**

That is a terribly bitter pill for many folks to swallow, because it means that you have to live the values and philosophies you espouse, day in and day out. The "do as I say, not as I do" approach does not work.

"The price of greatness is responsibility."
– Winston Churchill

Face it: as a leader, you live under a microscope—scrutiny comes with the job. By the very definition of the word "leader," you are supposed to be someone whom other people want to follow. To lead effectively, you have to have a personal commitment to leading people in the right direction; that is a very serious commitment indeed. Lead correctly—with honesty, clear values, integrity, and love—and you can make a dramatic positive impact on the lives of the people you lead. That opportunity to make a positive impact on people is the reward that comes with the responsibility of leadership. Remember: Everyone is watching you. Nothing you do is small.

Key Points

» Organizational excellence is a form of human excellence.

» You can't have a great team without great team members.

» Surround yourself with people who are smarter than you are.

» The foundation of great leadership is trust.

» 4 C's – Competence / Concern / Communication / Consistency

» C.C.C.T. – Courage / Candor / Clarity / Timeliness

» I am good at what I do, and I do it because I care about you.

» Everyone is watching—nothing is small.

"Our excellence never consists entirely in what we do alone or are, but rather in what we do with, or are, to others." – Tom Morris

5
Attitude Is Everything

"For success, attitude is equally important as ability."
– Harry F. Banks

Great leaders have great attitudes. They look for the positive; they focus on success and growth and learning. They are not Pollyannas, ignoring negative news or trying to make bad situations seem rosy. They are honest, frank, and realistic, but realize that their attitudes—in all situations— will have tremendous impacts on the attitudes of all the people around them.

"The good man chooses what is positive, what is advancing, embraces the affirmative." – Ralph Waldo Emerson

As I pointed out in the last chapter, your team watches every move you make; they hear what you say and don't say, see what you do and don't do, and look to you for clues and guidance about how they should feel, behave, and interact with each other. They literally follow your lead!

Have you ever worked in an office with a boss who did not realize the effect she has when she brings her bad attitude into the workplace? As she drives into the parking lot, everyone watches to see what the day will hold. When she steps out of her car, slams the door, and stomps toward the office with a nasty scowl, every person in the place runs for cover.

"Of all the things you wear, your expression is the most important." – Janet Lane

The Financial Impact

For the past several years, I have been leading advanced leadership training retreats for groups of executives from across the country. In these classes, I often ask people to describe the effect a leader with a bad attitude has on them and their work. Here are the answers I've received most often, from thousands of respondents:

"It makes mc hate going to work."

"I don't give my all, I do just enough to get by."

"The quality of my work suffers, I don't feel valuable."

"It sucks the life right out of you. You feel tired and drained and unmotivated."

"I spend most of my time trying to avoid my boss."

These comments strongly reflect the findings of a recent national survey, which revealed that as much as 50 percent of lost company productivity is a result of poor leadership. Put another way, you might be able to double your revenues by improving your leadership skills, abilities and, especially, your attitude.

Lest you think I exaggerate, two mammoth research studies were recently carried out by one of America's most respected polling organizations in which they interviewed more than one million employees and 80,000 managers— both pointed to one very powerful conclusion: **Great teams need great TEAM LEADERS.**

You can hire the best people, pay them well, shower them with generous benefits, and put them through exhaustive training, but the most important factor that determines an employee's productivity is that employee's relationship with his or her immediate supervisor. A single bad leader can kill an entire great team.

"The first great gift we can bestow on others is a good example." – Thomas Morell

"The only way leaders can make values tangible and real to followers is through their behaviors and actions. Employees look to their leaders as role models of how they should behave. And when in doubt, they believe action over words, without fail." – John W. Gardner

The Personal Impact

"The mind is its own place, and in itself can make a Heaven of Hell, a Hell of Heaven." – John Milton

I want to share with you something that is near and dear to my heart. As part of the leadership retreats I mentioned earlier, I also ask the attendees: "What is the personal impact on you and your family from your having to deal with a leader with a bad attitude?"

» "It makes me hate myself because I hate my job, but I feel powerless to do anything about it."

» "When I have a bad day – I go home and take it out on my family, I can't help it."

» "I am usually so upset from work that my life becomes a mess too."

» "It makes me angry and frustrated all the time, mostly at myself."

When I ask the opposite question, "What is the personal impact of having a great leader?," the answers are quite different.

» "When I feel good about things at work, I feel like I can do anything."

» "I am more confident and energized."

» "I feel more creative, ready to take on new challenges."

» "When I feel good, I want to go out and help others."

» "When I am happy at work, I am much more productive and bring that happiness home."

To communicate this information is one of the main reasons I wrote this book. Frankly, it scares me how few leaders realize the incredible impact their actions and words can have on the people they lead.

"Sometimes when I consider what tremendous consequences come from little thing—a chance word, a tap

on the shoulder, or a penny dropped in the newsstand–
I am tempted to think that there are no little things."
– Ralph Waldo Emerson

As a leader, you influence people's lives. Your actions, decisions, and words can either build people up or tear them down. You can play an amazing role in helping to give people happier, more successful and fulfilling lives for themselves and their families—or you can literally destroy them. I cannot state this strongly enough: **There are no little things when you are a leader.**

As a Leader, You Must DWYSYWD

Time and again, when workers around the world are asked to name the most important attributes in a leader they would willingly follow, there is one answer that stands out above all other responses:

People want a leader who will tell them the truth!

To become a great leader, from this moment forward, you must make every effort humanly possible to Do What You Say You Will Do (DWYSYWD). Tell the truth. Keep your word. Take responsibility. Lead by example. Doing these things is not easy, but doing them is the only way to become a truly excellent leader.

"There is a reason why 99 out of 100 average business men never become leaders. That is their unwillingness to pay the price of responsibility. By the price of responsibility I mean the hard driving, continual work...the courage to make decisions, to stand the gaff... the scourging honesty of never fooling yourself about yourself." – Owen D. Young

The Gap

In my experience, there is one skill that clearly differentiates excellent leaders from people who fail as leaders. I have seen this skill in play a thousand times in boardrooms and classrooms across the country.

Imagine that there is a tense situation. Something has gone wrong, and everyone is feeling the pressure. Tempers are high, people are upset or worried—and the entire team turns to the leader for guidance and direction.

Leader "A" loses it. He starts to yell and scream, pointing fingers and assigning blame. He is completely reactive, letting the situation take control of him and his emotions. Overwhelmed, he attempts to address the problem through intimidation, threats, and aggression.

Leader "B" reacts much differently. She is calm and thoughtful. She asks questions, gathers information, and asks for ideas. She focuses on fixing the problem, not on fixing the blame. She is not happy about the situation, but realizes that bullying her team will not help. She is empathetic to the feelings of her people, and gets them involved in finding the solution. She tries to keep a sense of humor and perspective, while moving toward a positive solution and using the situation as a learning experience.

What is the difference between the two leaders? The difference is what I call control of The Gap, that period of time between when something happens to you and when you choose how to respond to it.

This is actually the meaning of responsibility—**the ability to choose your responses**. As humans, we are apparently the only animals on earth that can think about what we are thinking about. (Think about that!). Unlike Pavlov's famous dogs, we have the ability to control our responses.

Some people, however, have not discovered this power—they feel that they are at the mercy of events and their environment. You know the type: if someone cuts him off in traffic, he immediately goes into a tirade of vulgarities. If someone at the office makes a comment that pushes his buttons, he goes on the warpath. If a small problem crops up on the team, he completely loses control. This type of person will never become a great leader because he cannot pass the first and most critical test: **To become a great leader of others, you** must first be a great leader of yourself.

"The great man presides over all of his states of consciousness with obstinate rigor." – Leonardo da Vinci

All great leaders have great self-control. In times of danger, confusion, and turmoil, they respond with vision and calm confidence that guides their people toward safety. When people are losing their heads all around them, excellent leaders take control and respond appropriately to situations. Exercising self-control is one of the most powerful roles that leaders must play for their teams.

The Ideal Leader

Being able to remain focused and rational in the face of disaster is not an innate ability; it is a learned skill. What great leaders know is that to be able to react this way under extreme pressure, they must have a very clear concept of the way they want to react before difficult situations ever occur.

When something goes wrong, great leaders

are not reactive—they are responsible. They don't do what they feel like doing, or what they think they can get away with, or what is easy—they do what they believe the ideal leader would do. They take control of The Gap and ask themselves, "What would an ideal leader do in this situation?" or "What would the person I want to become do?" Then they do those things.

At first this can be very challenging, especially when everyone is looking to you for answers. If you get comfortable with controlling The Gap and acting *as if* you were an ideal leader, however, eventually you *will become* an ideal leader!

This scenario presupposes one thing, however—that you have a very clear and specific mental picture of how an ideal leader would react, a picture that you can use as a guide for your reactions.

To develop your own model of an ideal leader, you must ask yourself questions such as: "What sort of demeanor do I want to have?" "How will I interact with others?" "What behaviors and skills will I demonstrate?" "How will I coach and lead the team in time of crisis?" "What will I say and how will I say it?" "What will I *not* do?" "What will be the long-term impact of my actions?"

After hundreds of workshops, I've noticed an emerging pattern. When people describe the qualities of an ideal leader, the words they use most often include:

calm   fair   empathetic

thoughtful   decisive   asks questions

honest   solution-oriented   sense of humor

This list is by no means complete, but it is a good start; these are the qualities you need to develop to become an excellent leader.

It is only when you have thought about the following questions, and answered them carefully, that you can stop yourself the next time a situation arises—before you have a negative or knee-jerk reaction—and ask: "What is the calm, thoughtful, empathetic response? How can I get the team to focus on the positive and help them learn and grow from this?" instead of "Who can I blame?"

"He who gains mastery over other men is strong; but he who gains mastery over himself is all powerful."
– Lao-Tzu

"Reason and judgment are the qualities of a leader."
– Tacitus

Questions

Many people do not understand the incredible power of questions. As a leader, one of the most important tools at your disposal is a well-worded question. Here are just a few reasons why questions are so critical to leadership success.

» **Questions beg for answers.** When someone asks you a question, it creates a strong feeling of pressure for the need to answer it.

» **Questions focus your thinking.** The nature of the question will control what you think about and how you think about it.

» **Questions get people talking.** An especially well-phrased question can open up the lines of communication and set the stage for productive dialogue.

» **Questions make you listen.** If you are serious about asking good questions that will give you excellent information, you will be serious about listening to the answers.

» **Questions can control the answer.** The way you word a question will determine the answer you will get. The key here is to think of what you want to hear the person say—the words you want to have come out of that person's mouth—and then craft a question that will get them to say those words.

» **Questions can get people to persuade themselves.** Who does a person believe above anyone else in the world? That's right—themselves. The goal, then, is to get the person to tell you what you want them to hear. Let them talk themselves into what you want them to believe.

» **Questions give you control.** Whoever asks the questions directs the flow of the conversation.

Let me give you an example. Have you ever heard a frustrated leader ask his team something like, "What is wrong with you people?" The answer comes back: "Well, we hate our jobs, we don't get paid enough, our work is boring, this company is terrible, our products suck, and you are a crappy boss!" Ask a bad question, and you will get a bad answer.

On the other hand, if a difficult situation arises and you say: "I know things aren't perfect, and I am not happy about the situation either, but how can we all pull together to fix this problem and learn from it so we can be sure it does not happen again? I need everybody's best ideas." A different type of question elicits a much, much different type of answer.

Great leaders think their questions through carefully, because they understand that there are no trivial questions—they realize that changing a single word can dramatically affect the answers they will get, and they know that the very future of their organizations will be directed by the questions they ask of their people.

"The quality of your life will be determined by the quality of your questions." – Anthony Robbins

Key Points

» Great leaders have a "can do" attitude.

» People will follow your lead.

» Poor leadership causes as much as 50 percent of lost productivity.

» Great teams need great team leaders.

» One leader with a bad attitude can destroy a high-performing team.

» As a leader, you change people's lives.

» DWYSYWD—Do What You Say You Will Do.

» People want a leader who will tell them the truth.

» To be a great leader, take control of The Gap.

» Become an ideal leader.

» The quality of your questions determines the quality of your leadership.

"When enthusiasm is inspired by reason; controlled by caution; sound in theory; practical in application; reflects confidence; spreads good cheer; raises morale; inspires associates; arouses loyalty; and laughs at adversity, it is beyond price." – Coleman Cox

6
Lifelong Learning

"An investment in knowledge pays the best interest."
– Benjamin Franklin

Outstanding leaders are curious. They have a strong desire to find out everything they can about how to achieve their vision, plans, and goals. They read, study, explore, and experiment in an effort to quench their insatiable appetite for knowledge.

"The only people who achieve much are those who want knowledge so badly that they seek it while conditions are still unfavorable. Favorable conditions never come." – Clive S. Lewis

I recently saw a quote from the CEO of $26.9 billion dollar company which sums this point up better than I can. When asked what it takes to be a successful leader, this gentleman replied that it takes four simple steps.

1. Know and develop yourself.
2. Know and develop the business.
3. Know, develop, and support your people.
4. Communicate.

Let's examine these steps in a bit more detail.

1. Know and Develop Yourself

Great leaders start with themselves in their quests to build incredible teams and organizations. They take their own personal development very seriously. This most demanding of leadership challenges has two main aspects, self-awareness and leadership skills.

A. SELF-AWARENESS

Great leaders strive first to know and understand themselves. They look deeply into their own souls, and face the reality of what they see. They examine their own values, beliefs, behaviors, and attitudes with eyes toward what will be required of them as leaders. Each of them makes an earnest pledge to work every day to grow, learn, and improve in self-leadership, in order to become the kind of person that others would willingly follow.

This is really the most critical message of the entire book: "If you want to be a great leader of others, you must first become a great leader of yourself." Take this message seriously, and take it to heart, because it is the very essence of outstanding leadership.

B. LEADERSHIP SKILLS

The second area of constant self-evaluation and improvement is in the fundamental skills of leadership. These skills include excellent communications (listening, asking questions, empathy, conflict resolution); visioning (brainstorming, strategic planning, goal-setting); consensus building (motivation, diversity, team building); risk-taking; coaching; etc. Understanding that these are the basic components of effective leadership and that they are learned skills, aspiring leaders practice to improve these skills daily.

Let me give you some statistics that will help clarify this point. How many self-improvement books (books that teach you to be more effective at your job or in your life) do you think average college graduates read per year after they get out of school? The answer is 0.5—only half of one book! Another report found that 88% of people quit reading by chapter three of every book they buy; that is appalling! People in my classes tell me they want to succeed, they want to make more money, they want to be leaders—yet statistics show that the vast majority of people are unwilling to do even the slightest bit of work to improve themselves.

If you want your life to get better, you have to get better.

"So with slight efforts, how should one obtain great results? It is foolish even to desire it." – Euripides

Here is a challenge. If you were to sit down

and read one book for self-improvement or career improvement every two months—just six books a year—you would be in the top 1 percent in the country! If you were to read one book every month—12 books a year—you would be in the top 1 percent in the world. Remember focus, discipline, and action—the touchstones for designing a life of excellence and becoming a leader of excellence.

"If these distracted times prove anything, they prove that the greatest illusion is reliance upon material possessions. We must search for some other coin. And will discover that the treasure house of education has stood intact and unshaken in the storm. The man of cultivated life has founded his house on a rock. You can never take away the magnificent mansion of his mind." – John Cudahy

2. Know and Develop Your Business

Only leaders who take their businesses seriously—whether those businesses are multinational corporations, small family-owned ventures, or non-profit organizations—will build successful enterprises.

As a leader, you must become a dedicated student of continual improvement. What are the trends in your industry? Who are the leaders? Who is your competition? How can you improve your products, deliver better service, make you customers happier? What will it take to be the best at what you do? What else do you need to know? Who can you ask for help? What must you do today to move closer to your vision—to your philosophy of excellence?

Great leaders think about these questions all the time. Do you?

The need to know and develop your business is one reason why it is so important to do something you really love. If you truly enjoy your job, all of this studying will not seem like work—it will be fun, and will actually add value and happiness to your life.

3. Know, Develop, and Support Your People

This topic echoes Chapter Four (Believe In People), but is worth exploring again. The success of your organization is determined directly by the success of your people.

It used to be that "leaders" merely controlled the operation of machines. If you wanted to improve the success of your company, you simply tried to get a higher level of productivity and efficiency from your machines, or you bought newer and bigger ones. Today, competitive advantage comes from the management of knowledge—in other words, people.

Excellent leaders care about their people, both as workers and as individuals. Leaders invest time and money in the development and personal growth of their people, and strongly support their people by telling the truth, treating people fairly, and showing them respect. True success in leadership comes from making other people successful—making them into leaders.

"The highest destiny of the individual is to serve rather than to rule." – Albert Einstein

4. Communicate

All great leaders have designed personal philosophies of leadership excellence—philosophies that determine how they want to live their lives and run their organizations. Based on years of study, personal experiences, advice from mentors, and extensive contemplations, great leaders have devised personal leadership styles that communicate their philosophies in everything they do and say. Great leaders become living examples of what they believe leaders should be.

» What you are speaks so loudly that I cannot hear what you say.

» People judge you by your actions, not by your intentions.

» What you do today will determine who you will be tomorrow.

These three quotes might represent the most important idea in this book: Leadership is not about tricks and tactics or motivation and charisma—it is about character. It is about who you are as a person, which then defines who you are as a leader.

"Thoughts lead on to purpose; purposes go forth in action; actions form habits; habits decide character; and character fixes our destiny." – Tyron Edwards

With that said, I hope you will look back over this book and use it as a guide to help you design your own personal philosophy of leadership excellence.

The characteristics of good, solid leadership that I have presented can serve you as a strong foundation. These are by no means the only characteristics you will have to develop to become a great leader, but they provide you with a very good start.

"A man's true greatness lies in the consciousness of an honest purpose in life, founded on a just estimate of himself and everything else, on frequent self-examinations, and a steady obedience to the rule which he knows to be right." – Marcus Aurelius

Key Points

» Dedicate yourself to lifelong learning. Be curious.

» In order to be a great leader of others, you must first be a great leader of yourself.

» Know and develop yourself.

» Know and develop your organization.

» Know, develop, and support your people.

» Have a personal leadership philosophy and communicate it in everything you do.

» What you are speaks so loudly that people cannot hear what you say.

"Destiny is not a matter of chance; it is a matter of choice. It is not something to be waited for; but rather something to be achieved." – William Jennings Bryan

Chapter Seven

Leadership Questions

I was just finishing a speech based on the information in this book to the board of directors of a $7 billion dollar bank. I had talked about a clear vision, the best people, embracing risk—all the key points—and had opened the floor for questions. Heads were nodding, the CEO looked pleased, and the vice president who had gone out on a limb to bring me in was beaming with pride.

Then, out of nowhere, an extremely well-dressed older woman—the director of the bank's operations in New York City—stood up and growled in a condescending tone, "This is nothing new, these ideas you've talked about are fundamental. We already know all of this!"

Where there had just been loud applause, a hush fell over the room. All eyes were on me.

"Yes, you are absolutely right," I replied. "These are the fundamentals of being an excellent leader and creating a design for excellence in your organization. And yes, I really have not told you anything especially new or different." She smiled broadly, sensing she had put me in my place.

"But," I continued in a polite manner, "may I ask you one important question?" She nodded. "Do you honestly do all of these things every day in your bank?"

There was a long moment of silence. She stared at me in disgust. "No. No, we don't. Actually, we have a lot of work to do. I guess we really do need to go back and focus on the fundamentals. You're right, John. Thank you."

"The knowing is easy; the doing is difficult."
– John Spence

As I told you in Chapter Five, questions are very powerful because they beg for answers and focus your thinking. Take the following 12 questions seriously, and be completely truthful in your answers. If you can answer yes to all of them, you are probably a very accomplished leader. Any question that you answer no, or are unsure about, indicates an area on which you need to work.

1. Do you have a clear, vivid, values-based, and compelling vision for where you want to take your organization?

2. Do you communicate that vision clearly and consistently with all of your people?

3. Have you backed up your vision with specific, measurable, agreed-upon, and time bound goals that allow you to delegate responsibility and empower your team?

4. Have you created a culture of urgency throughout your organization that strongly encourages people to take action and make the vision real?

5. Do you believe in, and constantly search for, new opportunities to succeed and improve— and help others to do the same?

6. Are you a catalyst for change, always working to keep your team focused on success and opportunity?

7. Do you personally embrace risk and encourage thoughtful risk taking by your team, allowing people to fail without fear of retribution?

8. Do you consistently demonstrate that you are working hard to increase your competence and that you truly care about your people, so that you can build a solid foundation of trust in your organization?

9. Do you believe that excellent communication is a cornerstone of leadership, and make a concerted effort to improve your communication skills every day?

10. Do you accept that your attitude will directly affect the attitudes and behaviors of your entire organization, and take that responsibility seriously, always setting a positive and enthusiastic tone?

11. Are you truly a serious student of self-improvement and leadership excellence, making a personal commitment to continual improvement and lifelong learning?

12. Are you a living example of what you want your followers to be?

The More Things Change, The More They Stay the Same

In the seven years since I wrote this book, much has changed in the world of business. The Internet has evolved from innovation to dominant driver of business worldwide. India and China are becoming global economic forces. In the United States, Baby Boomers are beginning to retire, while Gen Y and Millennial workers are changing many workplace rules. As I write this, oil is the highest price it has ever been ($99 a barrel), and value of the dollar is at its lowest. The big three American automakers are on the verge of bankruptcy, while most of our major airlines are emerging from it. These are just a few of the shockwaves occurring in global business markets; I don't think anyone has a clear idea of how business will evolve over the next 10 years.

For me personally, the last seven years have been a whirlwind of travel, research, and study. I have led seminars and workshops for both large and small companies around the globe, averaging 200 days a year traveling to Hong Kong, Germany, Austria, Japan, Latin America, and throughout the United Sates. I have maintained my pace of reading at least 100 business books a year and a dozen or more business magazines every month, and listening to over 30 audio books a year. I've had fun lecturing on strategy and leadership at top universities such as Cornell, Rutgers, Stanford, and the Wharton School of Business. And I have been honored to meet many of the most influential business, military, and political leaders in the world.

Considering everything that has changed and everything that I have seen in my work, however, I can confidently assert that the key characteristics of outstanding leaders are still just as relevant today as they were seven years ago. In fact, I think these keys to great leadership have never been more important!

Let me share with you some of the things I have learned since this book first came out.

The TEC Big Four

For the past several years, I have served as a re-source speaker to an organization called The Executive Committee (TEC) Group, which is part of Vistage International, the world's largest CEO network. Each month, in cities around the world, small groups of CEOs from non-competing companies gather for a day of learning and peer mentoring. During the past five years, I have led workshops on strategy and leadership for more than 400 CEOs and senior executives in the intensive and focused atmosphere of the monthly TEC meeting.

At the end of these sessions, I always ask for feedback. I specifically ask the CEOs to share the greatest challenges they currently face as leaders in their organizations.

I am astounded that more then 90 percent of the CEOs identify exactly the same four issues: poorly communicated vision; lack of open, honest, and courageous communication; acceptance of mediocrity; and lack of execution of the business plan.

Poorly Communicated Vision

I have heard so many leaders say, "John, I am very focused on the vision of our company; I think about it all day, it keeps me up at night, it is burned into my brain. But I'll bet if you talked to people in my company who are three levels down, they would have no clear idea of what our vision is or what it really means."

Vision was the first leadership topic I wrote about years ago, and it remains extremely important. It astounds me how often I encounter leaders who either have no clear vision of where they want to take their business or, if they do have such a vision, do not communicate it clearly to the very people who are responsible for implementing it.

Vision is fundamental. There can be no long-term or sustainable success in a medium to large business without a clear, vivid, compelling vision of the future of that business. Vision functions as a compass that guides key decisions and the allocation of resources. If you are not totally clear about exactly what you are trying to build, it will be almost impossible for you to decide what to focus on and what your real priorities are.

I was talking with a client the other day, and our discussion led me to an epiphany about the difference between two CEOs with whom I have been working. Both of these men are very bright, sharp, and analytical; they are masters of considering every detail and weighing every option as they carefully evaluate the pros and cons of their decisions. One of these CEOs makes decisions quickly and effectively, while the other often seems incapable of moving beyond analysis, continually poring over decisions and delaying even simple ones for weeks and sometimes months.

As I thought about what I knew about these two CEOs, suddenly the difference between them became obvious.

The first CEO, who is highly analytical but makes even major decisions quickly, has something that the second CEO does not—a very clear, detailed, specific vision of exactly what he is trying to create with his business. If I were to ask him to tell me where his business will be in 10 years, he would talk for two hours straight. He can describe precisely—down to the color of the paint in the bathrooms and the type of shrubbery in the parking lot—where he sees his company in a decade. Why? Because he carries in his head a vision of his company, a fully developed and exciting dream of what he wants to build. Because he sees the future so vividly, he has a clear benchmark against which to measure his decisions; he simply asks, "What must I do to move one step closer to my vision? Will this decision take me toward my vision, or away from it?"

The second CEO is equally as smart and talented and every bit as dedicated as the first. But if I were ask him where he sees his business in 10 years, he would say, "I'm really not sure, at around $80 million, I guess?" The difference is plain and simple: The second CEO is an awesome guy, but because he is not truly clear about what he is trying to create, he has nothing to use as a benchmark when making even the most routine decisions about business strategy. Because he does not have a strong, clear focus, he is unable to set major priorities or be proactive in his market. And since he cannot make key decisions, it is impossible for him to delegate responsibility for those decisions to anyone else.

With regard to focus, it is my experience that when leaders lack clear visions for the future of their businesses and therefore cannot make *big* decisions, they focus exclusively on *easy* decisions. In most cases, this means focusing on cutting costs and reducing expenses. While it's important to keep costs low and we know that numbers don't lie, this situation reminds me of the classic business axiom: *No business has ever used the single strategy of reducing costs as a sustainable growth strategy to dominate its market.* No, not even Wal-Mart; everyday low prices is simply one of their strategies. Wal-Mart is also the world's biggest spender on logistics and IT infrastructure; in those areas, they spend vast amounts of money to buy only the very best, and often the most expensive, equipment!

Some leaders tell me that they don't believe in "the vision thing," or that they simply do not have the time to work on something as vague as visions for their businesses. Nothing could be farther from the truth. A vision is not some meaningless schlock item that you create on a two-day retreat and post all over the office, never to look at again. A true vision is an exciting, focused, realistic, inspiring image of what you and your people are trying to accomplish together; it is the reason you come to work every day, the impact you want to make on the world, the kind of company and product you aspire to build. Your vision does not have to be a Nobel Prize-winning masterpiece of literature—it just needs to be something that everyone understands clearly, and is excited about. And because vision is so important, you don't have time NOT to work on it.

Once you have developed the vision, the next critical step is to communicate it clearly to all stakeholders. In every imaginable way, over and over again, you need to tell everyone involved about the vision and why it is important. In meetings; on conference calls; in front of customers; at lunch with employees; in formal reviews; in emails; at the annual meeting—every time, all the time, you must deliver clear, consistent messages about your vision. And when you feel you have talked about the vision so much that it's driving you crazy, your employees are only beginning to hear the message. You have to keep at it—keep telling the story, keep painting the picture, keep people focused on the prize.

Lack of Open, Honest, and Courageous Communication

Lack of a clear vision used to be the number one problem I saw with my clients, but has now dropped to number two behind lack of open, honest, and courageous communication. Poor communication is now the single biggest problem I deal with in client organizations worldwide. Why is this? One reason is because communication is extremely complex. I won't do the math here, but as soon as you have more than three or four people in an organization, the number of possible connections in the communication web mushrooms exponentially. With 40 or 50 people in an organization, the possibility of miscommunication becomes overwhelmingly vast. I am frankly amazed that anything ever gets communicated well in large organizations.

The solution to the problem of communication complexity is to make superb communication a top priority—to focus on it, train heavily in it, measure it, and reward those who do it well. Being a truly good communicator is a skill that can be taught and learned, although it takes practice and hard work. With time, however, it is possible for people to improve their communication skills, and so improve the overall quality and effectiveness of communications within organizations.

A new facet of communication has emerged as a trouble spot. Increasingly, I've noticed that people seem to be afraid to tell the hard truth. People lack the courage to speak up in meetings and put difficult issues on the table. No one wants to be the person who brings up an uncomfortable topic. This is a dangerous trend.

In every organization, it is the leader's job to talk about the things that other people are afraid to talk about. When the room is full of darting eyes and shifting butts, the leader must be the one to model courageous communication and open the discussion that everyone had hoped would stay closed. The leader also needs to support strongly any other members of the team who are courageous enough to deliver bad news or broach uncomfortable topics. If you shoot the messengers, soon you will not get any more messages—and once the flow of information fails, the company will not be far behind.

Acceptance of Mediocrity

"John, after being through this class, I now realize that I have a few mediocre people in key positions in my organization. Every day that I retain the mediocre people, they have a negative impact on all of the people underneath them." While this is a difficult situation to admit, it is a situation that plagues many of my clients. Many managers talk about excellence and give lip service to the importance of talent and "people being our biggest asset," but do they truly live up to these goals?

What is even more devastating is the impact that acceptance of mediocrity has on your top people. When your best employees—people who are superbly talented and honestly committed to excellence—see other employees doing mediocre work, completing projects late, leaving early, and getting the same pay and benefits as the top performers, one of two things happens. Either your top performers leave, or they simply give up and lower their standards to the level of the slackers. Why? Because they know their leaders are not serious about excellence.

A great saying cuts straight to the heart of this problem: "Once you start *accepting* mediocrity in your life, you become a *magnet* for mediocrity in you life."

Great leaders do not tolerate mediocrity. Great leaders set clear, ambitious, realistic goals and high standards, then hold people 100 percent accountable for always meeting those goals and standards. Refusing to accept mediocrity is difficult and takes discipline, but it's the only way to build a world-class organization.

Lack of Execution

For the past three years, I have been invited to be a guest lecturer on strategic thinking at a special event at the University of Pennsylvania's Wharton School of Business. Usually, there are about 120 senior executives in my class. During the session, I ask, "What percentage of the time do companies that have a clear vision and a specific plan to achieve it effectively execute to that plan?" The answer I get most often is 10 to 15 percent of the time. Wow, that is scary!

Failure to execute to plan is one of the biggest issues I face in all of my consulting and training assignments; it is what we refer to in our firm as the knowing-doing gap. Leaders of companies know what they are supposed to do, and they have solid plans for dominating their markets—but creating a performance-oriented culture of disciplined execution to implement their plans effectively seems to be a challenge that few can meet. That failure, by itself, is frustrating enough, but the financial implications of that failure can be staggering. Inability to execute to plan is likely responsible for the overwhelming percentage of lost revenues in most large organizations.

The solution to this dilemma is simple, but by no means easy; the only cure is *process*. The leader must put into place a detailed, well-defined, and repeatable process for identifying, clarifying, prioritizing, assigning responsibility, implementing, reviewing, and rewarding against specific goals and high standards of professionalism. Consistent and effective execution does not happen by chance.

While holding a two-day offsite meeting to create a strategic plan is a great idea, it is merely the first small step in a long and arduous process of making sure that the plan is communicated well and implemented effectively. Only with a highly-focused system of goal setting, monitoring, and managing can any leader hope to keep her people on track and successful in turning their business plan into business reality.

The greatest hurdles to implementing this process are your own employees. It has been my experience that when you remove all of the places for people to hide and actually hold people accountable for doing the work they promised to deliver, they rise up in anger and fear and attempt to subvert or destroy the process. Why? Because, for the most part, people equate monitoring and tracking as a way for managers to catch them doing something wrong and punish them.

Let me tell you a story about how to reverse that kind of thinking. Several years ago, I was leading a national sales meeting for one of my top clients. The

CEO was rolling out a new software system to help track and monitor the activities of his sales team. As the CEO stood at the front of the room and talked about the new reports, systems, and processes, the team's mood went from bad to worse. The expressions of the salespeople shifted from concern to fear to disgust. The team was about to erupt into full-blown revolt when the CEO said something that turned the mood around in seconds.

"Hey, hang on a second here. I want to make it clear this system is NOT about punishment; it is about help. We are not going to track you all year and then wait until your review and use it to beat you over the head and not give you a raise."

The CEO looked them in the eyes and continued, "We are putting all of these checks and balances in place so we can help you. We are going to monitor you closely so we can see the very first sign that you might be getting off track, so we can rush in with help and support and training and whatever else you need to keep from getting into trouble. We want to use this system to make sure you can maximize your commissions and make the most money possible. This is not about punishing you after you have failed—it is about making sure we are here to support you, so you never get into a place where you could fail."

This, then, is an important key to disciplined execution—creating a specific, measurable, repeatable process for helping your people successfully implement the plan and share in its rewards. Another important key is making sure that the people who will be directly affected by that process are involved in developing it. If people have a say in what the process will be, there is a much better chance that they will be more committed to the outcome and less resistant to change. Get your people on board early, ask for their best ideas and feedback, and build a process that makes sense to the people who have to implement it. All this advice sounds obvious, but it is not always heeded.

Summary of the TEC Big Four

So there you have it. If you were to ask several hundred CEOs and senior executives to identify their biggest business obstacles are right now, the overwhelming majority of their answers would include four issues:

1. Poorly communicated vision

2. Lack of open, honest, frank and robust communication throughout the organization

3. Acceptance of mediocrity

4. Inability to implement key ideas effectively

Does this sound familiar? If so, you are not alone—and you've got work to do!

Other Key Trends and Big Ideas

As I review my work over the last few years for other key trends, several more big ideas emerge.

First is the importance of learning to say NO.

The More Things Change, The More They Stay the Same

I have never before seen my clients stretched so thin. Everyone is trying to do much, much more with much, much less. It is scary to see how much pressure some of my clients are under; many managers are regularly working 70-hour weeks, arriving on Monday morning with 40 hours of meetings planned in addition to their regular duties. This schedule is completely insane.

What's more, people in organizations seem to have lost the ability to set priorities. I watch in meetings as new projects are added to lengthy lists of current projects, and when some poor soul asks, "Well, if this is now a priority, which one of the other projects do we push to the back burner?" and the boss replies, "None—they all have to get done, and the schedule will not be adjusted." This is beyond insane.

I am going to be completely clear: The world does not work that way. Given fewer people and resources, it is impossible to make everything a priority and insist that everything get done on time, on budget, and flawlessly. At some point, leaders must step back and decide when to say no. There are two reasons why saying no is so critical.

The first reason is the old saw that declares if you try to be all things to all people, you will end up be nothing to anyone. This saying is a cliché because it is true. Purely from a business standpoint, the cliché reflects a fundamental characteristic of successful companies—focus.

Study any of the major business research, and you will find a striking pattern—the best companies are experts at making their main things *the* main thing. These companies are superb at identifying their core competencies and unique value, and then setting the priorities of the entire organization around those key differentiators.

To put this point another way, the best companies are very good at deciding where they *do not* add value, identifying where they *cannot* be world class and where they are *not* unique—and saying NO to those things.

It was a huge wake-up call for me, personally, when I realized that deciding what NOT to do was actually one of the most powerful strategic deci-sions that any leader can make.

The second reason that being able to say no is critical is because good people will not tolerate insanity for long. If you pile on project after proj-ect and claim that they are all priorities, eventu-ally your brightest people will realize that you lack focus and are unreasonable—and then they will leave. People who are truly talented have options, and if they find themselves in workplaces full of frenzied workaholics who have no concern for life balance, they will move on to other places that do not allow this kind of lunacy.

Which brings me to my next big trend: It is a war for talent! I know I stressed this point all through this book, but I want to say it one more time: I honestly believe that talent is the future of business. We are very close to living in a time when all business success will revolve around the leader's ability to find, attract, develop, and retain top talent. Why? Because talent is the only real competitive advantage left.

In today's Internet-driven world, location often means nothing. Everyone has access to capital. Technological advantages sometimes last only a few days. Scale is meaningless in many industries. So the only thing you have left that truly differentiates your company is the quality of the people who work there. The people in research and development, the people who deliver customer service, the leaders who make good strategic decisions, your sales team, your human resources people—these are the people who will determine the future of your firm.

What does the war for talent mean to you as a leader? You must become a master at finding top talent. Many companies talk about talent, but very few make their organizations magnets for talent. Being a talent magnet means that recruiting is a top priority, focused processes are implemented, and systems, incentives, and rewards are created in order to attract the best people you can possibly find.

Once you can attract talented people, you must then create a culture that allows them to thrive, be challenged, feel like they are making a difference, and have fun—because this is what top talent really wants.

Yes, you need to pay your talented people well, but the truth is that they just want to make what is fair and reasonable compared with what any other people doing their jobs would expect. After that, their decisions to stay or go all depend upon your organization's culture—something on which you, as the leader, have a tremendous amount of impact.

A Final Gift for You

Let me end this second edition of the book by giving you a gift that I feel is extremely valuable.

For the past five years, I have been preparing to write a second book about business strategy. My research has been concentrated on uncovering a pattern of business excellence. At last count, I had analyzed about 140,000 pages on best practices and winning strategies, and condensed this information to a single page of bullet points. Yes, that's right—one page. I am not going to go into a lot of detail here, since that is what the next book is for, but I would like to give you a glimpse of what I have learned.

At the foundation of successful business strategies lie several givens. The first is that, at the very least, you must produce a high-quality product or service. If what you sell is not worth buying, no amount of good ideas or cool strategies will help you. All sustainable business success is built on delivering real value to the customer—period.

Another given is that you need to have a solid handle on all of the financial aspects of your business. I love the old saying that if you aren't managing cash flow, you won't be managing much for long. Even great companies with amazing products and services, loyal customers, and fantastic strategies have been driven to ruin and bankruptcy by poor financial management.

The last given is that change is inevitable.

Change is the name of the game. There is no one strategy that will carry your company forever. Markets shift; consumer preferences change; new competitors appear; technology advances—and so must you. Even though I can identify, right now, some solid strategies on which you should focus on as a business leader, there is no guarantee that these same strategies will still be relevant in 20 years—or even two years!

With all of that said, here are the top business strategies upon which every great company I studied were relentlessly focused:

1. A **vivid vision**, clear and well thought out, of what the company is trying to create

2. The **best people**, superior talents who are masters of collaboration

3. A **performance-oriented culture** that demands flawless operational execution, encourages constant improvement and innovation, and completely refuses to tolerate mediocrity or lack of accountability

4. **Robust communication** that is open, honest, frank, and courageous, both internally and externally

5. A **sense of urgency**, the strong desire to get important things done and never waste time on trivia

6. **Extreme customer focus**, owning the voice of the customer and delivering what customers consider truly valuable

After doing my research, I discovered that these six strategies stand out in bold relief. When I first looked at my list, I was disappointed that these strategies are so similar to the six key characteristics of outstanding leaders that I outlined in this book. I wanted to discover something totally new, to create a list that no one had ever seen before— but that would be ridiculous. It was inevitable that the two lists would be similar, because these are the concepts on which great leaders must focus in order to build great companies. If having a vivid, inspiring, and well-communicated vision for the future of the organization is the foundation of business success, then creating and communicating that vision must be fundamental to leading a company to greatness.

My gift to you is your homework: Review the six key strategies I have listed above, and give your company a brutally honest score between 1 and 10 for how well it addresses each of these strategies, every single day.

» If you have the strategy nailed and are honestly world class in that particular area—give it a 10.

» Very good, but with room for improvement—score a 7.

» Sometimes you do this thing well, sometimes you do it poorly—get a 5.

» Every now and then you are able to deliver on this strategy, but most of the time you do not—that's a 3.

» Looks nice on paper, but we almost never focus or deliver on that strategy—you score a 1.

So there you have it, my parting gift to you. Anywhere you scored seven or below needs some attention. Anything at four or lower is an emergency, and needs attention right away.

I am leaving you with more homework because by now, you understand that this is the role of the leader—to do more, to stay focused, to tell the truth, to help people succeed and, most importantly, to serve your customers, your shareholders, your communities, and, at the very highest level, your employees.

Leadership is not power or position; it is not a title; it does not automatically come with seniority. Leadership is an obligation to be a living example of integrity and service, of competency and concern, of honesty and love. These are the qualities that define true leadership.

I wish you great happiness and success -- John

John Spence

John Spence continues to work as a management consultant and corporate trainer while enthusiastically pursuing his passion for learning and teaching. He divides his time between delivering customized speeches and workshops to organizations that seek out his assistance; acting as managing partner of Flycaster & Company, a creative branding, design, and business improvement group; lecturing at major universities; and fly-fishing for trout in Colorado or bonefish in the Florida Keys.

John's areas of expertise include leadership, marketing and sales excellence, high performance teams, and business strategy. Among the clients that have turned to John for his deep knowledge of these subjects, as well as his unique ability to present these subjects in a straightforward and clear manner, are: Merrill Lynch; GE Capital; Kinko's; Alltel; PrimeCo; IBM; U.S. Navy; Pepsi; AT&T

Global Solutions; United Bank; The PGA Tour; Allstate; Frito-Lay; USDA; Verizon; Ford; and dozens of smaller private companies, startups, government and municipal agencies, and nonprofit organizations.

We strongly encourage your feedback, stories, and suggestions about the ideas you learned in *Excellence By Design: Leadership*. We are eager to hear from you about how this book has helped you achieve new levels of leadership excellence in your organization and your life. You may contact John directly through his website at:

www.johnspence.com

If you are interested in finding out more about how John might be able to assist you or your organization, please contact Sheila Spence by email at sheila@johnspence.com or telephone at 386-418-8870, ext. 102.

Through both of our businesses—John Spence LLC and Flycaster & Company—we offer a variety of services to professionals, including: workshops;

training seminars; keynote speeches; management consultations and coaching; advertising and branding strategies; and graphic design.

We sincerely hope that you enjoyed reading *Excellence By Design: Leadership* and found it a useful, practical, and applicable book. If you would like to provide copies to your friends, colleagues, or employees, Flycaster & Company offers bulk discounts and customized copies that feature a unique greeting and your organization's logo on the title page, as well as a personalized note and signature from John Spence.

Thank you for reading *Excellence By Design: Leadership*. We wish you great happiness and success, both in your business and in your life.

Sincerely,

The Team at Flycaster & Company

FLYCASTER & CO.